SYLVIA PORTER'S 385 TAX-SAVING TIPS

HOW TO PROFIT FROM THE NEW TAX LAWS

AVON
PUBLISHERS OF BARD, CAMELOT, DISCUS AND FLARE BOOKS

SYLVIA PORTER'S 385 TAX-SAVING TIPS: HOW TO PROFIT FROM THE NEW TAX LAWS is an original publication of Avon Books. This work has never before appeared in book form.

The author has attempted to ensure that all information in this book is accurate. However, errors can occur, rules and regulations regarding tax and other matters do vary from location to location and are changed from time to time. The final 1987 income tax forms and schedules and the updated official instructions had not yet been released by the Internal Revenue Service when this book was prepared. Therefore, the author and publisher disclaim responsibility for the complete accuracy of the text. And as is always mere common sense, the reader is cautioned to consult a qualified accountant or attorney regarding accounting or legal problems.

This book went to press on October 1, 1987
and reflects the pertinent tax law as of that date.

Prepared with the editorial assistance of Warren Boroson.

AVON BOOKS
A division of
The Hearst Corporation
105 Madison Avenue
New York, New York 10016

Copyright © 1987 by Sylvia Porter
Published by arrangement with the author
Library of Congress Catalog Card Number: 87-26922
ISBN: 0-380-89995-7

First Avon Books Trade Printing: December 1987

AVON TRADEMARK REG. U.S. PAT. OFF. AND IN OTHER COUNTRIES, MARCA REGISTRADA, HECHO EN U.S.A.

Printed in the U.S.A.

OPM 10 9 8 7 6 5 4 3 2 1

TABLE OF CONTENTS

INTRODUCTION

It's been called the Tax Reform and Full Employment for Accountants Act of 1986.

But that's a bit unfair, and I don't want to join the chorus of unwarranted criticism that has been aimed at the Tax Reform Act. The Act does make the system more equitable. No longer can the very rich get away with not paying their proper share of taxes by investing in limited partnerships, and deducting three or ten times the money they put up. The Act also sees to it that most economic decisions in the future will be made for economic reasons, not for tax reasons. Eventually, the Act will also help simplify the tax code. But make no mistake: As complicated as taxes were before, they're even more complicated now.

SOME IMPORTANT NEW WRINKLES

Thanks to tax reform, we now have all sorts of "phase-outs." So even though tax breaks are going, they're not quite gone yet. For example, you supposedly can't deduct "consumer" interest anymore. But actually, it's being "phased out": You can deduct 65 percent in 1987, 40 percent in 1988, 20 percent in 1989, 10 percent in 1990, and nothing in 1991. Phaseouts are all over the place, and fortunately they tend to follow the 65–40–20–10–0 sequence.

And now there are three kinds of interest:

1

1. as mentioned, consumer interest (what you pay when you're late sending a check to a credit-card company, what you pay on auto loans);

2. mortgage interest (on a first or second residence), fully deductible within limits; and

3. investment interest (when you borrow from your stockbroker against your investments), fully deductible within limits.

It used to be confusing enough when there were just two kinds of interest: what you paid (deductible), and what someone paid to you (income).

There are also three kinds of income now:

1. active income (what you get paid on the job);

2. portfolio income (what you get from stocks, bonds, and other investments); and

3. passive income (what you get from renting real estate, or participating in a limited partnership, formerly called a tax shelter).

The distinctions are important. Generally, you can't use losses from passive income (tax shelters) to wipe out taxes you would otherwise owe on your active income or portfolio income. (Naturally, there are phaseouts of these losses—and, to make things more complicated, a special exception for certain investors in rental real estate.)

Another complication: Now there are more "floors" than ever.

Example: Before you can deduct your medical expenses, you must first be able to list all your deductions ("itemize") on Schedule A, which is part of Form 1040. That requires that all of your itemized deductions total more than the "standard deduction" you're entitled to. (There's a glossary at the end of this introduction, in case you're unfamiliar with any terms.)

Today, only your total medical expenses that surpass 7.5

percent of your "adjusted gross income" can be deducted. The 7.5 percent is the "floor."

For casualty and theft losses to be deductible, you must first subtract $100; your losses must then surpass a floor of 10 percent of your adjusted gross income.

For a variety of other expenses (certain "miscellaneous" deductions), there's now a floor of 2 percent.

TWO BASIC TAX-REDUCING TACTICS

Your tax strategies must also change, to an extent, to deal with tax reform. Remember what Justice Learned Hand said: Tax avoidance isn't the same as tax evasion. You can do everything within your power to lower your taxes, by legitimate means. You can sell stocks that have gone down, to get a deduction, then buy the same stocks back (thirty-one days later). You can even buy U.S. Government EE savings bonds, and not report the interest until you cash in those bonds years later. But if you take a loss on those stocks, and secretly buy back the same stocks within thirty-one days, or if you never report the interest on savings bonds you've cashed in, you may be in a spot of trouble. You may be guilty of evasion.

Throughout this book, you will be told about a perfectly legitimate tax-avoidance strategy. It's called "bunching." It means pushing or pulling your deductible expenses into a target year.

Let's say that next year (Year Two), you plan to move to a new job, across the country. Your new employer won't pay you for the cost of the move. You can deduct the moving costs only if you qualify to itemize. Otherwise, the entire cost won't be deductible.

What you should do is try pushing your other deductible expenses from Year One into Year Two. That way, you'll almost certainly be able to itemize in Year Two. For example, if you receive medical or dental bills in December of Year One, pay them in Year Two. You can add them to your deductible expenses in Year Two. If you pull deductible expenses from Year Three into Year Two, you'll further boost your chances of being able to itemize in Year Two. Pay December's bills from Year Two in December. You'll also want to consider pulling income scheduled for Year Two into Year One, and pushing income scheduled for Year Two into Year Three. If it doesn't make much difference one way or another, sell a stock for a gain at the end of Year One, or at the beginning of Year Three. That way, your adjusted gross income in Year Two will be lower—and (a) you'll be more likely to be able to itemize, and (b) you'll be more likely to surpass the floors for deductions that are based on your adjusted gross income.

In short, this strategy calls for "bunching" as many of your deductible expenses as you can into one favorable year. But keep in mind that there may be complications: Your income in Year Two may unexpectedly shoot to the sky, for example (you might win a lottery); that means your adjusted gross income may rise, and so would all the floors you would have to surpass!

Another strategy—an old and honored one—that you should generally follow may conflict with the bunching strategy. But you should bear it in mind: Defer income, and take deductions now.

Let's say that you've written a paper on nuclear physics, or painted someone's house. The editor, or the person whose house you've painted, could pay you in December of Year One, or January of Year Two. Choose January of Year Two. If you choose December of Year One, you have to pay taxes on that income by April 15 of Year Two. If you choose January of Year Two, you won't have to pay taxes on that income until April 15 of Year Three. That's a whole year's grace! (But remember: You may have to pay estimated taxes on that money.)

Take deductions early for the same reason. If you're selling a stock for a loss, other things being equal, do it in Year One. That will lower the taxes you'll have to pay on

April 15 of Year Two. If you sell in Year Two, you'll lower the taxes you must pay in Year Three—and may get a tax refund a whole year later!

What should you do with that extra money? Invest it, spend it, whatever. The point is—it's almost always better to have money sooner rather than later. Money has a "time-value." The sooner you get it, the more valuable it is. If you receive money in January of Year One rather than January of Year Two, you could put it into a savings account and earn an entire year's worth of interest. Or you could buy a compact-disc player with the money, and enjoy the device for an extra year.

USING THIS BOOK

Here's how this book is organized: Chapter 1 and Chapter 2 lead you through Form 1040, with money-saving suggestions on what filing status to choose, how to lower your reportable income, ways to take advantage of credits, and so forth. Chapter 3 plunges into Schedule A, itemized deductions. Chapter 4 focuses on deductible medical expenses, Chapter 5 zeros in on casualty losses, Chapter 6 spotlights charitable contributions. From there, we go into more detail on various investments—securities (stocks, bonds, and such), insurance-based investments, and real estate (Chapters 7, 8, and 9). Then there are detailed suggestions for homeowners (Chapter 10), employees (Chapter 11), entrepreneurs (Chapter 12), parents and the divorced (Chapter 13), and retirees and people planning for their retirement (Chapter 14). Chapter 15 is devoted to the alternate minimum tax, a special tax for people who take advantage of too many tax breaks.

Appendix A gives the tax rates for 1987 and 1988; Appendix B is a chart detailing the facts about investing in mutual funds with and without insurance.

There's some overlap in the book: A suggestion that someone who is self-employed hire his or her child, for example, is suitable for both parents and for entrepreneurs. (But, to play fair, it's a numbered tip in one chapter, and tucked into another tip in a second chapter.) In some cases, I wasn't sure where to put a tax tip. For example, should the suggestion that you turn your hobby into a business go into the chapter for employees—or for entrepreneurs? I put it into the chapter on entrepreneurs.

So if you don't see an area that interests you, look at the detailed description of the chapter titles, or consult the index.

DON'T BE INTIMIDATED

Despite the fact that taxes are complicated, do try to do your own tax return yourself—if you have the time, if you have the inclination.

First, it will save you a tax adviser's fee. Second, you'll probably try harder than anyone else to shrink your tax bill. As the truism goes, no one cares more about your money than you do. Third, you'll keep up-to-date on the tax code— and thus in the future be able to make sure your financial dealings take best advantage of the tax rules.

If you're worried that you might make mistakes, for yourself or against yourself, you might take a stab at doing your own return, then have a tax preparer look it over.

Granted, some portions of the tax code seem to be written for people with IQs over 160. Or people who spend forty hours a week, year after year, doing nothing but studying taxes. The rules about depreciation, about the alternate minimum tax, even about summer home rentals, are dizzyingly difficult.

It's not you: It's the tax code. Almost everyone else is as perplexed as you are, and believe me, you won't be the first person if you make a mistake.

A woman, Barbara, recently told me that she would never be able to pay her tax bill for 1988. She had figured out what 28 percent of her income was, and it came to more than she could afford. I explained to her that not all of her income will be taxed at 28 percent; much of it will be taxed at only 15 percent. (The 28 percent tax bracket applies to only the top slice of her income.)

A minister, Tom, didn't know he could deduct his 1986 contribution to an individual retirement account from his total income, thus saving taxes on $2,000. He's since filed an amended return.

An insurance man, Bob, paid Social Security taxes, and so did his wife. Because of the overlap, he deducted her contribution, under "Payments." Wrong, Bob.

Other notable taxpayer mistakes:

- A man in Los Angeles deducted the cost of his daughter's wedding as a casualty loss. When an IRS agent phoned for an explanation, the man replied, in all seriousness, that his daughter's new husband had turned out to be a total disaster.

- Another California man phoned his local IRS office in frustration because he kept getting a negative amount on his tax return. As he told the IRS clerk, "The instructions said to subtract line 8 from line 7, and whenever I subtract 8 from 7, I keep getting minus 1."

- An Atlanta man was sure that he qualified for the foreign tax credit because he had resided in a foreign country the previous year: Alaska.

- A Miami woman, recently arrived from Cuba, had read in a newspaper that her children were worth more than $1,000 apiece as exemptions. She marched over to the nearest IRS office, two children in tow, and asked how soon she would receive her $2,000.

So . . . don't be intimidated. Try to do your own taxes. A lot of other people won't do as good a job as you can do.

PREPARING YOUR RETURN

At the outset, find out what extra forms you may need. Your library, post office, or bank should have them. And to make your task a bit less difficult, buy a simple, no-frills calculator—you can deduct the entire cost if you itemize and surpass the 2 percent floor for miscellaneous deductions.

How much time you will need to do your return depends, obviously, on how complicated it is. Several hours is probably typical. And even if you don't knock everything off in one sitting, at least have a goal every time you sit down with your tax forms: for instance, listing all your medical deductions, or all your capital gains and losses. Set aside a day or an afternoon when you know you won't be interrupted.

Begin by recalling everything significant that happened in your financial life last year. Did a storm topple a tree in your yard? Did your landlord keep your security deposit? Did you take a course to maintain your job skills? Did you have a face-lift or a hair transplant? These expenses are probably deductible.

To jog your memory, if you still have last year's calendar on which you marked appointments and special days, glance through it. Look for errands to help a charity, visits to physicians you may have lost the records for, and so forth. Naturally, you'll go through your cancelled checks, your insurance reimbursement forms, and your bills, too.

Now proceed to all the income, interest, and dividends you racked up last year. Assemble your W-2 forms, bank statements, brokerage-house forms, and so forth. And gather up your bank-deposit slips, upon which you should have indicated the sources of your money. (If not, start doing it now.)

Separate your deductions into categories—medical, taxes, moving expenses, and the like. Put your records into plain manila folders. And then plunge in—using this book to help you reduce the toll.

Remember that you can get an automatic four-month extension if you file Form 4868 before April 15 and pay what you estimate you owe. If you have a good reason, you can also get another two-month extension.

Finally, remember that you can round off numbers: If you have a figure like $50.50, you can make it $51; if it's $50.49, you make it $50.

DO YOU REALLY KNOW WHAT THESE WORDS MEAN?

One reason why taxes are so complicated is that the IRS uses unfamiliar words, or familiar words with special, unusual meanings.

If you study this list, in the future you may have less trouble understanding when the IRS talks.

Adjusted gross income: All your taxable income, minus a few "adjustments" like contributions to a pension plan. The adjustments are listed on the bottom of the first page of Form 1040.

Alternative minimum tax: A special tax reserved for high-income taxpayers who've managed to take too much advantage of tax breaks.

Basis: The cost of an item, when you calculate how much profit or loss you've made when you sell it. For example, for a stock, you add the broker's fee to the cost of the stock itself to find the "basis." On a house, you add improvements you've sprung for to the purchase price. A possible synonym for "basis": total investment.

Capital gains/losses: Profits or losses on the sale of stocks, real estate, or other assets held as investments.

Casualty and theft losses: Losses to your property or other assets because of a sudden, unexpected, unusual event, like a storm that blew in your windows. A casualty or theft loss may be deductible from your income.

Credits: Amounts you can subtract, dollar for dollar, from the income tax you would pay otherwise. Example: the credit for "the elderly or the permanently and totally disabled." Credits are better than deductions. Deductions are subtracted from your income, not from your tax bill itself.

Deductions: Subtractions from your adjusted gross income. If you're in the 28 percent marginal tax bracket, a deduction of $1,000 (for, say, medical expenses) saves you the $280 in taxes you would have paid otherwise.

Dependent: Someone you support and who entitles you to an exemption on your tax return.

Depreciation: A yearly deduction you can take on a business asset, like rental property, that supposedly loses value as it ages.

Earned income: Money from your job, as opposed to money from securities or from a limited partnership. Also called "active" income.

Estimated tax: Taxes you pay four times a year when the taxes withheld from your salary aren't enough to meet the total tax you expect to owe.

Exemptions: Everyone you support, including yourself. Each exemption reduces your taxable income, for 1987, by $1,900. Also called "personal exemption."

F.I.C.A.: Social Security tax.

Gross income: Your taxable income from all sources. (Interest from most municipal bonds, for example, isn't taxable, so it's not included.)

Head of household: An unmarried taxpayer who pays over 50 percent of the cost of maintaining a residence for another person for a year. A head of household is entitled to pay taxes at a special lower rate.

Itemizing: Listing all your deductions on Schedule A, as opposed to taking the standard deduction.

Joint return: A tax return filed by a husband and wife together, combining their incomes and deductions.

Lump-sum distribution: The payment an employer makes of the balance due you from a pension or profit-sharing plan. The entire distribution must be made within one year for it to qualify for special tax treatment.

Marginal tax bracket: The rate at which your last dollar of income is taxed. If you're in the 38.5 percent marginal tax bracket for 1987, your income is taxed at 11 percent, 15 percent, 28 percent, 35 percent, and finally 38.5 percent. (See the tax-rate table in Appendix A.)

Property: Real estate, or—as far as taxes are concerned— any asset you own, like stocks, a painting, or a car.

Rollover: A distribution from a pension plan, like an individual retirement account, that you reinvest in another pension plan within sixty days of your receiving the distribution.

Standard deduction: An amount you can deduct from your adjusted gross income if you don't itemize all your deductions. (For married people filing a joint return, the standard deduction is $3,760 for 1987.)

Support: Payments you make to care for a dependent, as for food, shelter, clothing, and medical expenses.

Taxable income: Your income, after subtracting adjustments, deductions, and exemptions, and before subtracting for credits and payments.

Chapter One
EVERYONE'S 1040

Yes, Form 1040 will look familiar. But because of tax reform, even on the top of the first page there are a few notable changes, among them:

• you no longer get extra exemptions for being blind or sixty-five or over;

• you no longer automatically get an exemption for yourself (if you can be claimed as a dependent on someone else's return, such as your parents' return, now you can't claim an exemption for yourself);

• you must provide the Social Security number of any dependent five years old or older;

• you must divide dependents into the number of children who lived with you, the number who didn't live with you (because of your divorce or separation), the number of your parents, and the number of other dependents; and

• you must now use an attachment to your return if you claim more than seven dependents. (Why the IRS picked seven is intriguing.)

This chapter will provide tax-saving suggestions, beginning with the whole process of filing your return and proceeding through listing your exemptions; the next chapter will pick up with reporting your income, and carry you through the amount you owe—or, let us hope, the amount of your refund.

FILING

1 GET PERMISSION TO FILE LATE.

You could be hit with a penalty if you cannot get your return in on time. But there's a simple solution: You can obtain an automatic four-month extension to submit Form 1040 (or 1040A) just by filing Form 4868 by April 15. But you must have paid all your taxes by April 15; submit what you estimate you owe with Form 4868.

You can get still more time to file your return, but only if you have a good reason. File Form 2688. Submit it early, to give the IRS time to consider your request. Good reasons: Your tax records were destroyed by fire, your tax preparer died or is ill, third parties (your employer, a bank, an investment adviser) failed to provide you with information you need to complete your return.

2 HAVE THE IRS FIGURE OUT YOUR TAXES.

Benefit: If you think you'll owe taxes, you may get a grace period. You must file by April 15, so go into your local IRS office just before that date. The IRS, of course, will need time to figure out what you owe. And once it tells you, you'll have thirty days to pay up, without being charged any interest. Yes, it's a bit sneaky, but if you're pressed for funds, you might consider it. It's certainly better than what some other taxpayers do—send a check that bounces, and get hit with a penalty!

Note, there are some requirements for having the IRS figure out your taxes for you. They are: Your income must consist only of wages, salaries, tips, interest, dividends, pensions, and annuities; your adjusted gross income (your total income minus things like contributions to pension plans) must be $50,000 or less; you don't itemize your deductions but take the standard deduction; you must file your return by April 15.

3 DON'T FILE A "FRIVOLOUS" RETURN.

You may get socked with an immediate $500 penalty if you submit a return that's clearly incorrect, or doesn't have sufficient information. Example: A taxpayer claimed two dependents and an incredible ninety-nine exemptions.

4 FILE A RETURN JUST TO GET A REFUND.

Even if you don't have to file a return (because you didn't have sufficient income, which depends on your filing status), submit a return for a refund. This might be the case if you worked part-time and taxes were withheld from your paycheck. Or if you are entitled to the earned-income credit. (See Chapter 2.)

FILING STATUS

5 FILE A JOINT RETURN EVEN IF YOUR SPOUSE DIED.

Usually, you will pay less taxes if you file jointly rather than singly. And if your spouse died on January 1, you can still file a joint return for the rest of the year. By the same token,

6 FILE A JOINT RETURN IF YOUR SPOUSE DIED WITHIN THE PAST TWO YEARS.

You can enjoy the lower tax rates of filing jointly for two years following your spouse's death, provided

- you could have filed a joint return with your spouse during the year of the spouse's death, even if you didn't;
- you have not remarried; and
- you have furnished over half the cost of maintaining a home that was the main residence of a dependent son, stepson, daughter, or stepdaughter.

Once two years have elapsed, you can claim head-of-household status. (See Tip Eight.)

7 CONSIDER FILING SEPARATELY FROM YOUR SPOUSE . . .

if the two of you earn about the same amount of money, and if one of you had very high medical expenses . . . or large, uninsured casualty losses . . . or employee business expenses . . . or if you're getting divorced (the higher-income spouse can deduct alimony payments, the lower-income spouse will pay tax on the money at a lower rate) . . . or if you live in a community property or marital property states (Arizona, California, Idaho, Louisiana, Nevada, New Mexico, Texas, Washington, or Wisconsin).

But while you may sometimes save taxes by filing separately, your gain may be offset by the loss of the child-care credit. (See Chapter 2.) You'll have to do some calculating.

8 CONSIDER FILING AS A HEAD OF HOUSEHOLD.

You'll pay less in taxes, usually, than you would if you filed singly. Your tax rate may be lower, your standard deduction higher, and—unlike single people—you may be able to use the earned income credit. To qualify, you must

- be unmarried or legally separated under a divorce

decree or a separate-maintenance agreement on the last day of the year;

• pay over half the cost of keeping up the main home of a parent, whom you can claim as a dependent (you needn't live with the parent);

• pay over half the cost of keeping your own home, which was the year-long home of one of the following: (a) your unmarried child, grandchild, foster child, or stepchild (none need be your dependent); (b) any person listed below whom you CAN claim as a dependent (except under a multiple-support agreement): grandparent, brother, sister, stepbrother, stepsister, stepmother, stepfather, mother-in-law, father-in-law, brother-in-law, sister-in-law, son-in-law, daughter-in-law, and (if related by blood, not marriage) an uncle, aunt, nephew, or niece.

9   FILE AS A HEAD OF HOUSEHOLD IF YOU'RE MARRIED . . .

but living apart from your spouse. Rules: You must file a separate return, you must pay more than half the cost to keep up your home, your spouse didn't live with you at any time during the year, and your home was the main residence of your child or stepchild, whom you can claim as a dependent, for over six months of the year.

10   CLAIM HEAD-OF-HOUSEHOLD STATUS EVEN IF YOUR CHILD DIDN'T LIVE WITH YOU . . .

if you have two homes, some distance apart, and your child lives in the one you consider your main residence, for which you pay more than half the upkeep—even if you spend only 40 percent of your time there. A court ruled that 40 percent was adequate.

11 REMEMBER: YOU DON'T HAVE TO LIVE WITH YOUR PARENT.

You can be the head of a household, and your parent can live apart, in a hotel, house, apartment, or hospital.

12 MAKE SURE THAT YOUR PARENT QUALIFIES AS YOUR DEPENDENT.

You must contribute more than half your parent's support to claim your parent as a dependent—and your parent cannot have earned more than $1,900 a year in 1987. If you give your father $5,000 to stay in an apartment, and he used $5,000 (mostly from his savings) for his own support, he is not your dependent, and you cannot qualify as the head of a household. Giving him $1 more would have turned the trick.

13 FILE FOR HEAD-OF-HOUSEHOLD STATUS EVEN IF YOUR PARENT DIED DURING THE YEAR . . .

or if a child who made you eligible for head-of-household status was born during the year. You qualify so long as you maintained the person's chief residence during the part of the year he or she lived with you.

14 INCLUDE DOMESTIC HELP AS A COST OF HOUSEHOLD UPKEEP.

To figure out whether you provide half the cost of a household, also include property taxes, mortgage interest, rent, utility charges, repairs and maintenance, property insurance, and food eaten in the residence.

PERSONAL EXEMPTIONS

15 CLAIM AS MANY EXEMPTIONS AS YOU CAN.

They're worth $1,900 apiece in 1987; $1,950 in 1988; $2,000 in 1989. And they qualify as deductions from your taxable income—without annoying floors of 2 percent of your adjusted gross income, 7.5 percent, or 10 percent (for, respectively, miscellaneous deductions, medical deductions, and casualty deductions). You are entitled to a personal exemption for yourself and your spouse; you're also entitled to a dependency exemption for someone you support, such as a child.

But high-income taxpayers are losing the personal exemption. Beginning in 1988, their $1,950 exemption is being phased out. For single taxpayers, the phaseout begins when their taxable income reaches $89,560. For married taxpayers, the benefits decline once income reaches $149,250. For heads of household, it's when income reaches $123,790.

These exemptions will be eliminated by means of the special 33 percent tax rate, which eats away at the value of the personal exemption once your income climbs above the levels mentioned above.

Also, if you claim a child as a dependent, the child can no longer use the personal exemption on his/her own.

16 MARRY IN DECEMBER, DIVORCE IN JANUARY.

If you marry in December, you can file as a married couple for the entire current year, which usually lowers your taxes. If you divorce in January, you can file jointly for the previous year and claim your spouse as an exemption. (No, I'm not suggesting that the SAME couple marry, then divorce, just for tax reasons. The IRS would raise the roof.)

If your incomes are similar, though, you might be better off marrying in January, divorcing in December. Another reason to switch the months: if neither of you can itemize. Individually, you can each claim a higher standard deduction if you file separately.

Of course, let's not overlook strong emotional and romantic considerations from these calculations!

17 REMEMBER THE HIGHER STANDARD DEDUCTION FOR THE BLIND AND SIXTY-FIVE OR OLDER.

You can no longer get extra exemptions if you're blind, or sixty-five or older. But now you're entitled to a higher standard deduction—in 1987, the blind get the higher 1988 standard deduction, which is $3,000 ($5,000 for joint filers). For others, the standard deduction in 1987 is only $2,540 for singles, only $3,760 for joint filers.

A joint filer who is elderly or blind is entitled to an extra standard deduction of $600 ($1,200 if both spouses are elderly or blind, or one is elderly while the other is blind). A single person gets an extra $750 deduction for being elderly or blind—$1,500 if both.

18 CLAIM THE HIGHER DEDUCTION FOR BLINDNESS IF YOU CAN'T WEAR CONTACTS.

Even if your eyesight would improve if you wore special contacts, you will be considered blind if the contacts cause pain or ulceration, and you can wear them only briefly (and regular glasses wouldn't help). If you are totally blind, meaning you cannot tell light from darkness, attach a note to your return. If you are partially blind (your vision is no better than 20/200 in your better eye, even with corrective lenses), attach a note from a physician or optometrist declaring that you are medically blind.

DEPENDENTS

19 CLAIM A FRIEND AS A DEPENDENT.

You can, if

- during 1987, your friend's gross income was under $1,900, and in 1988, it was under $1,950;
- you furnished more than half your friend's support;
- your friend used your home as a main residence;
- your friend lived in your household for the entire year (temporary absences, such as for vacations, don't count).

Similarly, you can also claim as a dependent a member of the opposite sex who is living with you and whom you are supporting—providing that, in your state, such a common-law arrangement isn't illegal.

A person qualifies as your dependent if

a. you furnish more than half the person's support (but see Tip 33);

b. the person's total or gross income isn't $1,900 during 1987, unless he/she is under nineteen or, if over nineteen, a full-time student;

c. if not a close relative, the person was a member of your household and lived with you the entire year. (Close relatives, who don't have to live with you, include: child or legally adopted child, grandchild, great-grandchild; stepchild; brother, sister, half brother, half sister, stepbrother or stepsister; parent, grandparent, or other direct ancestor; stepfather or stepmother; a brother or sister of your father or mother; a son or daughter of your brother or sister; your father-in-law, mother-in-law, son-in-law, daughter-in-law, brother-in-law, or sister-in-law.)

d. The person must be a citizen of this country, or a resident of this country, Canada, Mexico, the Canal Zone,

or the Republic of Panama during the year—or an alien child
adopted by and living with a U.S. citizen abroad.

   e. The person does not file a joint return with a spouse—
unless the couple files merely to receive a refund.

20 CLAIM A CHILD THAT DIED AS A DEPENDENT.

While you can't claim a stillborn child, you can claim a
child that lived even briefly.

21 HAVE A BABY IN DECEMBER, NOT JANUARY.

One accountant I know argues that, by having a baby at the
very end of the year, you get a dependency exemption for
the eleven preceding months. (Talk about planned parent-
hood!)

22 OBTAIN A SOCIAL SECURITY NUMBER FOR EACH DEPENDENT.

You must list the number on your return. You'll need one
for any child who is at least five by the end of the tax year.
Otherwise, there's a $5 penalty.

23 CLAIM AN ILLEGITIMATE CHILD.

24 TAKE A DEPENDENT WHOM YOU DIDN'T SUPPORT FOR THE ENTIRE YEAR.

If your child, say, moves out during the year, you can still
claim the child as a dependent if you provided over half of
the child's support. The length of time doesn't matter; the
amount you spend does.

25 INDICATE WHICH OF TWO PARENTS YOU SUPPORT.

Let's say that you contribute $6,500 to your parents' support. They spend $12,000 on their own support. The IRS would hold that you gave each parent $3,250. That, plus half of $12,000, means that their individual support consisted of $9,250. And your contribution of $3,250 is NOT over half of $9,250. But if you had indicated in a note that your $6,500 went to only one of your parents, and had given checks only to that parent, your $6,500 would have been over half of the $9,250—and you could claim that one parent as a dependent.

26 BE WARY OF CONTRIBUTIONS THAT DON'T COUNT AS SUPPORT.

Support doesn't include your payments of income taxes, Social Security taxes, or life-insurance premiums. It does include cash, food and lodging, maid service in the home, education, medical and dental care, recreation, transportation, and "similar necessities." Thus, if you pay for someone's expenses of driving a car (oil, gas, insurance), that counts as support. If you give someone a TV set for that person's exclusive use, include its fair market value.

27 DON'T OVERLOOK WEDDING EXPENSES IN CALCULATING SUPPORT.

Wedding apparel and accessories, the wedding reception, and flowers for the wedding party, the church, and the reception count toward support. So do music lessons, dancing lessons, books and supplies, clothing, laundry, dry cleaning, telephone bills, summer camp, baby-sitters, entertainment (like toys and movie tickets), vacations, and charitable contributions made on behalf of the potential dependent. Furniture, appliances, and cars may also count.

28 PERSUADE A POTENTIAL DEPENDENT TO EARN LESS.

Let's say that your father has earned $1,000 in 1988, working part-time. You've contributed $1,950 toward his support. Once he earns over $1,950, you will lose him as a dependent—both because his total income is too high, and because you haven't contributed over half his support. Suggest that he cut down on his work, in return for your increasing your support.

29 PERSUADE A POTENTIAL DEPENDENT TO SPEND LESS.

Let's say that you might claim your father as a dependent except that he uses too much of his savings or income to support himself; suggest that he save more of his money, or give more to your own children. If your father saves his money, or gives it away, it doesn't count as self-support. So you might more easily qualify as contributing over half of his support.

By the same token, persuade a potential dependent child who's working part-time to save or invest some of his/her money, too, so it will be easier for you to contribute over half of his/her support.

30 USE THE FAIR RENTAL VALUE OF A ROOM, NOT YOUR ACTUAL COSTS.

If a potential dependent lives with you, calculate the cost of the lodgings as what a renter would pay—not your proportionate expenses. Take into consideration the use of furniture and appliances, the cost of heat, electricity, and water. You'll usually make out better that way, because the fair rental value should include a margin for profit as well as a reserve for future repairs and maintenance.

31 DON'T INCLUDE THE VALUE OF SCHOLARSHIPS AS SUPPORT . . .

if the child is a full-time student. Thus, if you contribute $4,000 to a child's support, and the child has only a $4,000 scholarship, you're considered to be contributing ALL of the support.

32 DON'T INCLUDE SOCIAL SECURITY IN A DEPENDENT'S GROSS INCOME.

The maximum total income that a dependent can have in 1988 is $1,950—unless the dependent is a child under nineteen or a full-time student. But if an adult receives Social Security payments, you needn't include it in figuring his or her gross income. Still, if the adult spends the money to support himself or herself, you'll have to take the amount into consideration in calculating whether you passed another test—that you provided enough to claim the dependency exemption.

If your potential dependent receives Medicare reimbursements (Part A) and reimbursements for physician care (Part B), you can also exclude them in determining whether you provided more than half the person's support. The IRS contends, however, that Medicaid payments for the poor do constitute support.

33 PERSUADE A POTENTIAL DEPENDENT TO GET TAX-FREE INCOME.

If your parent has $1,950 in income from corporate bonds, you cannot claim him or her as a dependent in 1988. But if part of the investment income came from municipal bonds, the interest wouldn't count toward the $1,950 barrier. So persuade your parent to invest in munis—especially considering that, recently, they were paying almost as much as corporate bonds and Treasury obligations. Other nontaxable income that doesn't count toward the $1,950: life insurance, gifts, and inheritances.

34 IF YOU RECEIVE HELP WITH SUPPORT, DECIDE WHO WILL BENEFIT MORE FROM THE EXEMPTION.

Let's say that your mother gives you money to support your child. You and she should decide who should claim the child as a dependent. If you're in a higher tax bracket, you might be better off claiming the exemption. In that case, make sure that your mother's contributions are given to you to use as you wish—not for the child. Otherwise, she should make out her contributions to you with a note on her checks, "For support of child."

If you are divorced or separated, you can work out such an arrangement with the other parent. Generally, the parent who has custody of the child can claim the child as a dependent. But if the other parent would benefit more, tax-wise (the other parent might be in the 28 percent bracket, while you're in the 15 percent), you can work out a deal. If you're the custodial parent, you can give the other parent a declaration (Form 8332) that you won't claim the child as a dependent, so the other parent can—by attaching the declaration to his/her return. (Note: A pre-1985 written agreement might have given the exemption to the parent who didn't have custody if that parent provided at least $600 for the child's support during the year.)

Still another situation: You, your brother, and your sister contribute equal amounts to a parent's support. None of you can claim the parent as a dependent—unless the three of you file a multiple-support agreement, allowing just one of you to claim the dependency exemption. What you might do: Alternate claiming your parent as a dependent year by year.

Any person who furnishes over 10 percent of the support can claim the exemption, if the others agree to it. You'll need Form 2120.

35 TAKE A MARRIED CHILD AS A DEPENDENT . . .

if you provide more than half the child's support, the child's income isn't over $1,900 (for 1987), and the child and her spouse don't file a joint return (except to obtain a refund). Because you're probably in a higher bracket than your child's family, you'll benefit more.

36 TAKE A FULL YEAR'S DEPENDENCY EXEMPTION FOR SOMEONE WHO DIED.

You can do this even if the person died early in the year.

Chapter Two
DEEPER INTO 1040

Form 1040 has other significant changes. Now, you must report your tax-exempt income—from municipal bonds, for example. And you don't deduct $100 (or $200, if filing jointly) from your stock dividends. You don't pay taxes on just 40 percent of your long-term capital gains, but on 100 percent.

Moving expenses are no longer an adjustment to your income; you can deduct them (if you pass the usual tests) only if you itemize on Schedule A. That's where employee business expenses are now, too. And the deduction for a married couple who both work has vanished.

Gone too is the partial credit for political contributions.

Still, around 90 percent of Form 1040 is just the way it was before tax reform.

INCOME

37 DEFER INCOME
IF YOU CAN.

If you're scheduled to receive any income late in the year, it's usually better to receive it early the next year instead. You'll have an entire year to spend or invest all that money

27

without having to pay taxes—apart from whatever estimated taxes you might be required to fork over. The later in the year you're owed the money, the better it would be to defer getting it. If you could have received the money EARLY in the year, you'll miss out on what the money could have earned for you during the first part of the year.

Still another reason to postpone income: You may be in a lower tax bracket next year. Heaven forbid, but you may lose your job, or be disabled, or suffer a terrible business loss. That's less likely to happen THIS year, simply because this year is partly over. (Besides, tax brackets in general are heading down in 1988.)

Naturally, if you expect to be in a much HIGHER tax bracket next year—because of raises or bonuses, or selling property or other assets—disregard the previous advice. Pull income into this year, not next.

To defer income, ask an employer to hold off paying you for some work until early next year. But ask him or her BEFORE you perform the project, or the IRS will object. And get it in writing, in case you don't trust your employer. If you're thinking of working overtime, postpone the extra work until early next year.

Self-employed? Postpone sending out bills for November and December until late in December or early in January.

38 DON'T REPORT TAX-FREE INCOME.

Such as:

• the value of any health-insurance policy your employer pays for you
• damages you receive from a personal-injury lawsuit (your doctor operated on the wrong knee, a neighbor made malicious remarks about you)
• premiums your employer paid on the first $50,000 of term life insurance for you, providing that all employees get

the same treatment; premium payments on whole-life insurance that your employer paid IF the benefits are lost if you leave your job (term is plain insurance; whole life comes with a savings account)

- gifts you receive, or money you inherit
- life-insurance proceeds when you're the beneficiary
- money you receive from a health-insurance company to pay your medical bills (you subtract the money from your medical deductions)
- scholarship money you receive for tuition and other course-related expenses, like books, supplies, and equipment if you're working toward a degree (scholarship money for room, board, and incidentals is now taxable—unless the scholarships were granted on or before August 17, 1986, or on or after August 17, 1986, if you received the proceeds before January 12, 1987, to pay expenses incurred before that date)
- supper money your employer pays if you must work overtime
- the expenses that a would-be employer pays for you to come for a job interview
- unemployment insurance if you purchased the protection yourself (but not if your employer paid for it)
- prize money that you donate to charity
- employee awards for length of service and job safety (up to $1,600 a year per employee, and up to $400 for a nonqualified awards plan), and traditional retirement gifts
- small gifts your employer may present you with, like a turkey at Christmas, or the use of the photocopying machine, or having a secretary type something personal for you
- free services your employer provides when it doesn't cost him or her anything extra (like free flights to airline employees, free phone service to telephone company workers)
- reasonable discounts your employer gives you on goods or services
- money your employer provides to cover the cost of

having someone care for your child or other dependent, thus enabling you to work (the person providing the care cannot be a dependent of yours, or a child of yours under nineteen); if the care is outside your home, it must cover a child under fifteen, or a dependent or spouse who is incapacitated and spends at least eight hours a day in your house

• money your employer provides for tuition for your taking courses related to your job

• the cost of meals that your employer provides, if the meals are supplied at your employer's place of business and for his or her convenience (so you can be called upon for help even while you're biting into a hamburger), or if you're allowed only a short time to eat (up to forty-five minutes)

• a place to live that your employer provides on the business premises for his or her convenience, if you're REQUIRED to live there (but if you have a choice of free lodging on the premises or a rental allowance for living elsewhere, and you choose the former, the value of the lodging is taxable income)

• free parking your employer provides for you at or near the office, business use of a company car, and subscriptions to business magazines your employer provides

• contributions that your employer makes to your government-approved pension plan (like a 401 [k] plan)

• Social Security taxes your employer pays for you if you're a domestic worker or an agricultural worker

• strike payments if they're made to both union and non-union workers, the payment varies in accordance with a person's needs, you needn't do anything in return for the payment, and at the time you're not getting unemployment compensation or other government help

39 DON'T INCLUDE THE FULL COST OF A BOOBY PRIZE.

Let's say that you win, as a prize, a trip to Tijuana in the heat of summer, or bedroom furniture that might have been fashionable in 1942. So long as the prize has flaws, or strings attached (you must use it within a certain time), you needn't report its supposed selling price as income. Just report what you consider its fair market value—what someone might actually pay for it. Check around to see if anyone might buy it from you, and at what price.

40 KEEP FROM HAVING TAXES WITHHELD IF YOU WON'T OWE ANY.

If you work only a short time for modest wages, you probably won't owe any taxes—though taxes may automatically be deducted from your salary. Give your employer Form W-4, certifying that you owed no Federal taxes last year and don't expect to owe any this year.

41 DON'T REPORT AS TIPS WHATEVER WAS A PURE GIFT.

Here's an imaginary example: You're a waitress in a restaurant. A patron comes in, doesn't sit down, tells you that you remind her of her long-lost daughter, and gives you $100. Then she leaves. That's not a tip—it's a pure gift.

INTEREST YOU RECEIVE

42 DON'T REPORT INTEREST ON . . .

tax-exempt state and local bonds; an individual retirement account, Keogh plan, pension plan, or profit-sharing plan so long as you don't make any permanent withdrawals. (But remember: Beginning with 1987 returns filed in 1988, you must list your tax-exempt interest. If you have a lot, be prepared for the IRS to inquire how you obtained the money to buy the bonds.)

43   MAKE SURE YOUR TAX-EXEMPTS ARE REALLY TAX-EXEMPTS.

Beware of certain "private activity" bonds, the interest from which is taxable as of September 1, 1986. Such bonds usually pay more than general-obligation bonds. And beware of even tax-exempt private-activity bonds—such as those to finance airports and sewage facilities—because their interest will be considered a tax-preference item, subjecting you to the alternate minimum tax. (See Chapter 15.)

44   MAKE SURE THE PAYER HAS YOUR CORRECT SOCIAL SECURITY NUMBER.

If not, you'll face penalties, and the payer can withhold 20 percent of your interest in the future. Look carefully at the 1099-INT statement you receive.

45   DON'T LIST INTEREST UNTIL YOU RECEIVE IT.

Don't report the interest on a certificate of deposit if (a) it matures (becomes payable to you) next year, and (b) its maturity isn't over a year, and (c) interest isn't credited and can't be withdrawn except at maturity. Example: You buy a one-year CD in February 1988, and you receive your investment plus interest in February 1989. Report the interest in 1989, not 1988. The same goes for Treasury bills that mature next year.

46   DON'T DECLARE ALL INTEREST YOU'RE SUPPOSED TO HAVE RECEIVED.

Examples: interest a bank or other financial institution credited to you but that you didn't really get because the institution was insolvent. (Some state-insured banks still haven't paid interest they owe from years ago.) Also, interest you supposedly received, according to a Form 1099-INT, may be incorrect. Let's say you bought a bond, and paid the seller for "accrued interest"—the interest he/she is owed between payment periods, all of which will automatically go to you. When you receive Form 1099-INT, report the total interest on your return, and subtract what's known as the "purchased interest."

If you're receiving interest from insurance proceeds from a life insurance policy on your late spouse, who died on or before October 22, 1986, you can exclude $1,000. This remains true even if you remarry.

47 HESITATE BEFORE USING YOUR CHILD'S SAVINGS FOR THE CHILD.

If you've given money to a child under a law like the Uniform Gift to Minors Act, don't use any of the income to support the child, else it will be taxed to you. In some states, you have a legal obligation to pay for your child's college education if you can afford it, so be careful about invading your child's assets even for that reason.

48 ROLL OVER YOUR SAVINGS BONDS.

You have a choice about reporting the interest on a Series E or EE government savings bond. You can report it year after year (few people do), or report the total interest when the bond matures. And there's a third choice: When the bond matures, you can make a tax-free exchange of the proceeds for another government bond (HH)—or just keep your bond beyond the maturity date, still collecting income. That will continue to postpone the date you must declare the interest you've accumulated.

Old Series E bonds have a final maturity of forty years after they were issued: They are immediately taxable then.

49 HAVE YOUR CHILD REPORT INTEREST ON SAVINGS BONDS IF . . .

the child is fourteen or older, and has very little income. The child's standard deduction may wipe out any tax due on the interest. If the child waits to report the interest, he or she may be in a higher tax bracket when the bonds mature. (Much of the income of children under fourteen, remember, will now be taxed at their parents' highest rates.) The same strategy would hold for anyone who has very little income.

DIVIDENDS

50 DON'T REPORT INSURANCE "DIVIDENDS" AS DIVIDENDS.

They're a return of premiums you paid that were more than the insurance company needed. As for the "dividends" you received from credit unions and savings and loan associations, they're really interest, and should be reported as such. Distributions made by money-market funds are really interest on short-term obligations, but you do report them as dividends.

What ARE dividends? They're the money you receive because of your ownership of a corporation's stock. As mentioned, once upon a time, $100 ($200 if you filed jointly) was untaxed. No more. Still, dividends are nice to have—and not just because they're worth more now that tax rates are going down. They also provide some protection against a stock's going down too far and too fast. Generally, a stock paying a 5 percent dividend won't plummet as much as a similar stock paying a 3 percent dividend— because the more a stock goes down, the higher its yield (the dividend in conjunction with the stock's price) becomes, and the more attractive it is to investors interested in high income. (Of course, there's a danger that a company in really bad shape will reduce or eliminate its dividend.)

51 NOT ALL DIVIDENDS ARE TAXABLE.

A "return of capital" isn't taxable. What this means is that you're just getting back part or all of what you invested. If a dividend is really just a return of your investment, it's not taxable. Your Form 1099-DIV should indicate as much. But keep in mind that a nontaxable dividend lowers the basis (the purchase price, for tax purposes) of your investment. If you invest $100, get $50 back as a return of capital, then sell the stock at $50, you don't have a $50 capital loss. You've broken even.

"Liquidating" dividends are also nontaxable. They're issued by companies going out of business, and at least part of what you receive will be just a nontaxable return of your investment.

Another instance where dividends aren't taxable: when you receive stock or the right to buy stock as dividends. The rules: You cannot choose to receive cash instead; and the stock isn't preferred stock—which pays higher dividends and has first claim over "common" stock if a company goes bankrupt.

TAX REFUNDS

52 DON'T REPORT STATE AND LOCAL TAX REFUNDS . . .

if you didn't itemize (list all your deductions on Schedule A). Reason: You didn't deduct for those taxes, so you've already paid your full federal tax on those refunds.

If you paid the alternate minimum tax in a previous year, you might not have to report a state or local tax refund, either: In calculating the alternate minimum tax, you weren't allowed to take deductions for state or local taxes.

ALIMONY RECEIVED

53 DON'T REPORT ALIMONY UNLESS...

your ex-spouse can deduct the payments on his/her return. The ex-spouse cannot deduct them if they aren't made in cash, and if you and your ex live in the same households. Another rule: If annual payments exceed $10,000, they must continue for at least six years—unless the person receiving the money remarries, or either person dies. (See Chapter 13 for more on alimony.)

54 DON'T CONFUSE CHILD SUPPORT WITH ALIMONY.

If you receive child support, you needn't declare it as income, and your ex-spouse cannot deduct it. (Still, your ex-spouse might be able to claim an exemption for the child.) Property settlements are also not considered taxable alimony. (For capital gains and losses, see Chapter 7; for pensions income, see Chapter 14.)

SOCIAL SECURITY

55 CONSIDER NOT MARRYING.

If you and another person are receiving Social Security benefits, and have been planning to marry, you might think again—depending on your sense of morality. You might be better off, tax-wise, by not marrying. Perhaps this isn't so amoral as one might think; at your age, sudden illness could prove financially devastating, so you must think especially hard about money matters.

The reason you should consider not marrying: A married couple filing jointly will begin paying taxes on their Social Security benefits if their combined income is $32,000 or more. But two single people can each have incomes of $25,000 before their benefits are taxed—for a total of $50,000.

An accountant I know would even counsel two married people with combined incomes over $32,000 to get divorced. It's probably better than another alternative: that, while married, they not live together and file separately. In that case, the benefits of each spouse also wouldn't be taxed until they reached $25,000 apiece.

56 INVEST IN TAX-DEFERRED INVESTMENTS.

If you don't need the extra income immediately, consider buying growth stocks, those that pay low dividends or none at all; or buy Series EE savings bonds, and skip paying taxes on the interest until they mature or you cash them in. These tactics will lower the threat that your Social Security income will be taxed.

57 ALTERNATE GOOD YEARS AND LEAN YEARS.

Just as other taxpayers should consider bunching their deductions into alternate years, someone at risk of paying taxes on Social Security benefits might bunch income into alternate years—so that, during one of those years, he or she avoids the full tax. Sell stocks for gains in one year, for example; sell stocks for losses in another year. Buy Treasury bills and certificates of deposit with interest that's taxable the next year, when they mature.

OTHER INCOME

58 REMEMBER WHAT INCOME ISN'T TAXABLE.

Some taxpayers are TOO conscientious. Or they just don't know the rules. Examples of nontaxable income:

• the value of fruit and vegetables you grow and consume yourself
• insurance payments (for your wrecked car, for instance)
• debts you owed that were canceled as a result of a gift (example: You owe a parent $500; he/she tells you to forget it. But if the debt was canceled because the lender simply despaired of ever collecting, you must report the forgiven balance as income).
• forgiveness of student loans because you worked for a specified time in certain professions for certain employers (for instance, a young doctor's loan might be forgiven if he or she worked for two years in a rural area).

Other income that you normally needn't report: life-insurance proceeds (unless the insurance was an "endowment" policy, which simply paid you for your investment—not for life insurance); health-insurance payments (unless you received a flat amount per day, not direct coverage of your expenses); Veterans Administration benefits; cost-of-living allowances if you work for the government; public-assistance payments; payments under a workers' compensation policy; insurance payment for the loss of a limb; insurance payment for additional living expenses because your residence was destroyed; allowances someone receives from a parent or spouse (no, a child doesn't have to report a $5-a-week allowance); rebates that auto makers and others give to customers (they're really just reductions in the sales price); and, as mentioned, personal-injury awards (like money you receive from a successful libel suit, or for surrendering custody of a minor child). For other nontaxable income, see Tip 38.

59 DON'T INCLUDE PROPERTY EXCHANGES AS BARTER INCOME.

Barter exchanges must be reported by both participants. Example: You paint someone's house, he or she gives you legal advice, and no money changes hands. He or she must report the value of having his or her house painted; you must report the value of the legal advice. If you belong to a bartering club, and members exchange their services, you should receive Form 1099-B.

But an exchange of property isn't bartering. Bartering calls for the exchange of personal services.

Let's say that you trade your big old car to someone for her small new car; no money changes hands. So long as you clearly haven't made a profit on the deal, you needn't report any income. What if you trade a house for someone else's house, and the other house was worth far more than your house's basis (your total investment)? You can postpone paying taxes on the gain. (See Chapter 10.)

Other income you SHOULD report: all unemployment compensation (as a result of tax reform); jury pay (but not a mileage allowance for commuting to the courthouse; and if you gave your jury pay to your employer, because he/she paid you your regular salary, you can take a deduction if you itemize); partnership and S corporation income; royalties; hobby income; gambling winnings, though you can deduct your losings on Schedule A, up to your winnings (keep a record of all your losses, lest you win big at the end of a losing year); ill-gotten gains, as from embezzling, kickbacks, something that the IRS calls "push money," or bootlegging (if Al Capone had only paid attention!).

ADJUSTMENTS

60 ADJUSTMENTS ARE WORTH FAR MORE THAN DEDUCTIONS.

Actually, adjustments ARE deductions—but gold-plated ones. The differences between them and itemized deductions are:

a. Adjustments reduce your gross or total income directly. Deductions may be subtracted later on, after your gross income has been reduced by adjustments, and becomes "adjusted gross income."

b. You can always subtract adjustments from your income. But you can subtract deductions only if you itemize—and itemizing is becoming more and more difficult because the standard deduction is climbing. (See Chapter 3.)

Obviously, one reason why adjustments are better is that you can always use them, whereas you can use deductions only when you itemize. The other reason why adjustments are better: The bigger your adjustments, the lower your adjusted gross income. And the lower your adjusted gross income, the easier it will be for you to itemize all your deductions, as well as to climb over the floor to deduct medical expenses (7.5 percent of your adjusted gross income), the floor for casualty losses ($100 per occurrence and 10 percent of your adjusted gross income), and the floor for miscellaneous deductions (2 percent of your adjusted gross income).

Alas, there aren't many adjustments left. Moving expenses have just moved over to Schedule A, as an itemized deduction, though without the floor of 2 percent of your adjusted gross income. And UNreimbursed employee business expenses have also turned into an itemized deduction, WITH a floor of 2 percent of adjusted gross income.

What's left?

• Reimbursed employee business expenses. If your boss pays you for using your car on the job, you report the payment as income—and you can subtract the cost as an adjustment to your income. You're expected to come out even.

• Penalties you pay when you withdraw a time-deposit account early (for example, you put money into a certificate of deposit for a year, pull out the money after six months, and the bank hits you with a penalty).

• 25 percent of the health-insurance premiums you pay if you're self-employed (the remainder can be claimed as an itemized deduction).

• Alimony you pay. Remember to give your ex-spouse's name and Social Security number. (See Chapter 13.)

• Finally, deductible contributions to IRAs, to a Keogh retirement plan for the self-employed, and to a Simplified Employee Plan if you're self-employed. It's here that you can beef up your adjustments. Give as much as you can afford to your tax-deductible pension plans! And that advice applies to salary-reduction plans (like 401[k] plans) as well, because they provide the equivalent of adjustments to your total income, too. (See Chapter 14.)

CREDITS

61 REMEMBER: CREDITS ARE WORTH MORE THAN ADJUSTMENTS OR DEDUCTIONS.

A dollar's credit is worth a dollar of taxes saved. But adjustments and deductions don't reduce your taxes dollar for dollar—only up to 38.5 cents on the dollar in 1987, 33 cents in 1988. Whereas credits are subtracted from the taxes you might owe otherwise, adjustments and deductions are subtracted from your taxable INCOME. The meaning of all this: Nail down your credits!

Credits that ordinary taxpayers should pay special attention to: for child- and dependent-care expenses; for the elderly or for the permanently and totally disabled; and the earned-income credit, which is listed under PAYMENTS on Form 1040. Others: for foreign taxes, and a general business credit.

62 DON'T OVERLOOK THE CHILD-CARE CREDIT.

You are entitled to the child- and dependent-care credit if you provide more than half the cost of maintaining a household that includes at least one individual who qualifies you for the credit—and if you have expenses related to your employment that you must pay in order to keep your job.

The credit can be up to $720 if you have one qualifying person in your household, $1,440 if you have more than one.

The qualifying individuals must be one of the following:

a. a person under fifteen whom you can claim as a dependent, or whom you COULD claim if he or she didn't have $1,900 or more of income (in 1987—in 1988, it's $1,950;

b. a dependent who cannot care for himself or herself (you MUST actually claim this dependent, unlike the case above);

c. your spouse, if he or she cannot care for himself or herself.

How much can you claim? If your adjusted gross income is $10,000 or less, your credit is 30 percent of up to $2,400 of employment-related expenses—if you have one qualifying person in your household. If you have two or more qualifying individuals in your household, your credit is 30 percent of up to $4,800.

For every $2,000 that your adjusted gross income climbs over $10,000, the 30 percent drops 1 percentage point. So, if your adjusted gross income is $28,000, you can claim only 20 percent of up to $2,400 or $4,800—a maximum of $480 or $960. Here's how the percentages work out:

Adjusted gross income over . . .	Credit Percentage
$10,000	29%
12,000	28%
14,000	27%
16,000	26%
18,000	25%
20,000	24%
22,000	23%
24,000	22%
26,000	21%
28,000	20%

Employment-related expenses include:

a. household services, such as for a housekeeper, cook, or maid, but not for gardeners or chauffeurs—and not, the IRS notes, for bartenders. (Did anyone ever try to claim a credit for a bartender's expenses?)

b. out-of-household services, such as the cost of a day-care center or a similar arrangement. A day-care center must have state or local approval; your dependent must spend at least eight hours in your household—he or she cannot spend almost all day at the center.

Important rules:

• Educational expenses don't qualify if the child is in the first grade or higher; only nursery or kindergarten schools are eligible.

• Any expenses count toward your credit only if they enable you to keep a money-making job; if you do volunteer work for little or no pay, forget it.

• Your expenses can't be more than your income from

your job if you're not married at the end of the year—otherwise, why work? If you ARE married at the end of the year, your expenses must be LESS than the earned income of you or your spouse, whichever is lower.

• If you (or your spouse) are a full-time student, or disabled, you are considered to have $200 of earned income for every month you're not working because of studying or disability—if there's one qualifying person. The income is $400 a month if there are two qualifying people. The disabled person can be the spouse. Why the $200/$400 arrangement? So you can deduct more of the employment-related expenses.

• You can take the credit for expenses to pay only certain relatives to keep house for you, or take care of your dependents or your spouse. To qualify, these relatives cannot be claimed as dependents by either you or your spouse. (If they could, there would be lots of room for abuse—older brothers would be "paid" for taking care of younger brothers.) The relatives who qualify: a son or daughter nineteen or over at the end of the year; stepson or stepdaughter; brother, sister, stepbrother, stepsister; father, mother, or an ancestor of either (grandparents, typically); stepfather or stepmother; a son or daughter of your brother or sister; a brother or sister of your father or mother; a son-in-law, daughter-in-law, father-in-law, mother-in-law, brother-in-law, or sister-in-law.

• If you're married and living apart, you can claim the credit on a separate return only if (a) you maintain a household, (b) furnish half the cost for the year, (c) it's the main house of your child or other qualifying person for more than half the year, and (d) your spouse is absent for the last six months of the year. If you're divorced or legally separated, only the parent with custody of the child can get the credit. If you're married and living together, you can get the credit only if you file a joint return.

63 HIRE A PARENT TO CARE FOR YOUR CHILDREN . . .

if your parent isn't a dependent. This way, you can claim the child-care credit (if you meet the other rules), give your parent some extra money, and provide your child with loving care.

64 CLAIM THE CREDIT EVEN IF YOU WORK ONLY PART-TIME.

But remember that your employment-related expenses cannot exceed your earned income.

65 SEND YOUR CHILD TO SUMMER CAMP.

The expense will qualify for the child-care credit, so long as it's not unreasonable (don't choose a golfing camp). And, of course, your child must be under fifteen, and having the child at the camp must enable you to work.

66 CLAIM THE CREDIT EVEN IF YOU'RE OUT OF WORK . . .

providing that you're actively looking for a job.

67 DON'T SPLIT UP THE EXPENSES AMONG YOUR CHILDREN.

Let's say you have a housekeeper clean your apartment while your fourteen-year-old and your eighteen-year-old are in school. Use the full cost of housekeeper; don't apportion the expense between your eligible and ineligible children.

68 TAKE MEDICAL EXPENSES AS A CREDIT.

If there's any amount that's beyond the maximum, use it as a medical expense—if you itemize, and if you can climb above the floor of 7.5 percent of your adjusted gross income. Don't try taking the expenses as a medical deduction, then use the 7.5 percent you can't deduct as a child- or dependent-care credit. It's not permitted. (But a clever idea.)

By the way, not all of a child's medical expenses qualify for the child-care credit, such as routine medical or dental checkups.

69 DON'T OVERLOOK THE CREDIT FOR THE ELDERLY.

It can be worth $1,125 against your tax if you and your spouse are sixty-five or older. Overall, you may be entitled to a credit equal to 15 percent of the first $5,000 of your annual income. (Use Schedule R to figure out the credit.)

Even if you're under sixty-five, but you retired on permanent and total disability and your disability benefits are not tax-exempt, you may be entitled to this credit. You must have a physician complete the statement on the bottom of page 1 on Schedule R, attesting to the extent of your disability.

The flat amount you may be entitled to is reduced by

a. the nontaxable portion of your Social Security benefits, plus other tax-free retirement benefits; and
b. your adjusted gross income, or earned income beyond certain limits.

You won't be entitled to any credit if

• you're single, a head of household, or a qualifying

widow or widower, and you receive nontaxable Social Security or other nontaxable benefits of $5,000 or more, or have an adjusted gross income of $17,500 or more.

• you're married, filing jointly, and only one of you is qualified for the credit—and together you have nontaxable benefits of $5,000 or more, or an adjusted gross income of $20,000 or more.

• you're married, filing jointly, and both of you are qualified for the credit—and together you have nontaxable benefits of $7,500 or more, or an adjusted gross income of $25,000 or more.

70 DON'T OVERLOOK THE EARNED-INCOME CREDIT.

This credit is available to low-income workers with a child claimed as a dependent. To be eligible, you must maintain a household for yourself and the child; the child must earn less than the dependency exemption ($1,900 in 1987, $1,950 in 1988), unless the child is under nineteen or a full-time student; and if you're married, you must file a joint return.

For 1987, the credit is 14 percent of your earned income up to $5,714—for a total of $800. As your income increases (starting at $6,500), the credit is phased out. At the $14,500 level, the credit vanishes.

You don't need a special form to claim the credit, but the IRS mails out a worksheet.

71 FILE FOR THE EARNED-INCOME CREDIT EVEN IF YOUR TAX IS ZERO.

You'll STILL get the entire amount of the credit. (Yes, there IS negative income tax.)

72 GET THE CREDIT IN ADVANCE.

If you're sure you qualify, have your employer pay you the credit in your regular wages, by reducing any taxes withheld. Get a copy of Form W-5.

PAYMENTS

73 DON'T OVERPAY YOUR SOCIAL SECURITY TAXES.

You might—if you had two or more employers, and both withheld Social Security (FICA) taxes. The most you should pay for 1987: $3,131.70 on an income of $43,800. Either take the excess as a credit on your tax return, or—if one of your employers mistakenly withheld more than $3,131.70— have your employer make up the difference in your next paycheck.

It's possible to apparently earn less than $43,800 and still have too much Social Security taxes withheld.

A man I know had two jobs in 1986, when the top salary subject to Social Security tax was $42,000. Both of his jobs provided salary-reduction (401[k]) plans. So even though the combined salaries reported on his W-2 forms indicated that he had earned less than $42,000, he had paid more than the $3,003 limit in 1986. Reason: Social Security taxes had been deducted from the portion of his two salaries that he had salted away into his 401(k) plans.

REFUND/AMOUNT YOU OWE

74 IF YOU OWE $1 OR UNDER, FORGET IT.

But even if you're sure you'll owe less than $1, you must file a return.

Chapter Three
ITEMIZING

The IRS doesn't want you to list all your deductions on Schedule A. It's much more work for the IRS. To tempt you not to itemize, the IRS gives you an alternative: taking a fixed amount, the "standard deduction," instead. And to further tempt you, the standard deduction (formerly known as the zero bracket amount) is going way, way up.

	Standard Deduction	
Filing Status	1987	1988
Married, filing jointly and widows/widowers	$3,760	$5,000
Married, filing separately	1,880	2,500
Heads of households	2,540	4,400
Unmarried singles	2,540	3,000

There's another advantage to taking the standard deduction: You're less likely to get into trouble with the IRS. Taking the standard deduction means that the IRS won't question any write-offs you take for medical expenses, for casualty losses, for a home office, and so forth.

This chapter will cover itemizing in general, taxes you've

paid, interest you've paid, and miscellaneous deductions. Medical expenses, casualty deductions, and charitable contributions will be covered in the next three chapters. And despite the IRS, we suggest that you

75 TRY TO ITEMIZE.

If you think that your itemized deductions will exceed your standard deduction, itemize. You have the money coming to you. Do a rough calculation of your deductions. Do they exceed the standard deduction? If they do, but by only a tiny amount like $5, you might stop there. But if it's a few hundred dollars, consider going for it. There's a wonderful, little-recognized benefit to itemizing, besides any extra money you can collect: You'll become more familiar with the tax rules about deductions. And that knowledge can help you save money year after year.

You MUST itemize under certain circumstances—for example, if you're married, file a return separately from your spouse, and your spouse itemizes on his/her return.

76 DON'T SUBTRACT THE STANDARD DEDUCTION FROM YOUR ITEMIZED DEDUCTIONS.

A natural mistake. In 1986, you would deduct the zero bracket amount from the total of your allowable itemized deductions. Reason: The tax tables had been adjusted to include the zero bracket amount. But the new tax tables don't have the standard deduction built in.

Subtract your allowable itemized deductions directly from your adjusted gross income. Take the number of exemptions you're entitled to, worth $1,900 apiece for 1987, $1,950 apiece for 1988. Then consult the tax tables to see how much you may owe—or how much Uncle Sam may owe you.

TAXES YOU PAY

77 DON'T THROW AWAY YOUR SALES-TAX RECEIPTS.

True, sales taxes are no longer deductible. But they add to the ''basis'' (cost, for tax purposes) of whatever you buy. If an item you purchase (an antique, a Mercedes, a painting) grows in value and you sell it, you can subtract the sales tax you paid from your taxable profit.

78 PERSUADE YOUR MORTGAGE HOLDER TO PAY YOUR PROPERTY TAXES EARLY.

If you think you can itemize this year, and the bank that collects your mortgage also pays your property taxes, ask to have the payments scheduled for January paid in December. A tax deduction in hand is usually better than one in the bush. But if you definitely cannot itemize and thus deduct your real-estate taxes for the current year, forget it. Of course, if you pay your real-estate taxes directly, not through a bank, it will be easier for you to pay your property taxes this year or next.

79 DEDUCT STATE ESTIMATED-TAX PAYMENTS FOR NEXT JANUARY . . .

if you actually make the payment this December, and you think you can itemize this year. (The day you mail or deliver your check is generally the date of payment.) Of course, you have nothing to gain by making your January *Federal* estimated-tax payments in December.

80 DON'T OVERLOOK OTHER DEDUCTIBLE TAXES.

Besides property taxes and state and local taxes, you can deduct

- personal-property taxes (example: the fee your state may require you to pay for a license for your car, based upon the car's value)
- additional state and local taxes you may be assessed as the result of an audit or an amended return
- foreign income taxes (actually, you may be better off taking them as a credit—see which way yields a lower tax; in any case, you can't deduct them if you take advantage of the foreign earned-income exclusion)
- your contributions as an employee to state disability funds in California, New Jersey, New York, or Rhode Island, as well as to the Alabama unemployment compensation fund and the Washington State supplemental workers' compensation fund (examine your salary check, and add up your total yearly contributions)

81 FILE A JOINT RETURN WITH YOUR SPOUSE . . .

if you pay the real-estate taxes, but your spouse owns the house. If you file separate returns, you will lose the deduction on your return.

82 DON'T DECLARE A RENT REBATE.

Let's say that you're a tenant, your landlord receives a tax rebate, and he or she generously passes along part of it to you. Don't include it as income. As a tenant, you haven't been able to deduct your rent, so a tax rebate isn't a return of any deduction you took. By the same token, you need not report a state or local tax refund if you didn't itemize in the year the refund was for.

83 DEDUCT YOUR SHARE OF THE TAXES . . .

if you own a cooperative apartment. Tax reform, by the way, has given cooperatives more flexibility in how they apportion real estate taxes and interest among tenant-share-holders.

84 DEDUCT MORE THAN JUST TAXES ON YOUR CONDO.

You also pay your share of the taxes on elevators, corridors, swimming pools, and other "common" areas. Make sure that these taxes are added to the taxes you pay for your individual unit.

85 DEDUCT LOCAL TAXES FOR MAINTENANCE AND REPAIR OF STREETS.

If the taxes were for improvements (widening, lengthening), though, all you can do is add the taxes to the basis (cost, for tax purposes) of your property. This will lower your taxable gains when you sell your residence.

86 DEDUCT STATE AND LOCAL TAXES ON FEDERALLY EXEMPT INTEREST.

If (say) you live in California, and own a (say) South Carolina municipal bond, Uncle Sam won't tax you on the interest from that bond. But California will. Don't make the mistake of thinking that if California does, you can't deduct the California tax on your Federal return.

87 CHECK TAXES WITHHELD FROM YOUR FOREIGN INVESTMENTS.

If your stockbroker is holding the securities for you, he or she may not be informing you that foreign taxes have been withheld from payments to you. If that's the case, consider adding the extra interest or dividend income to your income, and taking a tax credit—which may be worth more than the additional tax you'll pay on the extra interest.

INTEREST YOU PAID

88 PAY INTEREST THIS YEAR RATHER THAN NEXT.

The amount of "consumer" interest you can deduct is dropping. In 1987, it was 65 percent. In 1988, it's 40 percent. In 1989, 20 percent. In 1990, 10 percent. And thereafter, nothing. (Consumer interest is interest on: credit cards; auto loans even if you, as an employee, use the car for business; student loans and such—not mortgage interest, not investment interest, not business interest.) So if you owe money on a credit card or have other consumer debts, try to pay them off in 1987 rather than 1988, 1988 rather than 1989, 1989 rather than 1990. (But if you'll be able to itemize in one year, and not the year before or after, do further calculations to determine when to pay the interest.)

If you're reading this before the end of 1987, you have another good reason to nail down interest deductions now. Your tax bracket may fall in 1988—say, from 38.5 percent to 33 percent or 28 percent or even to 15 percent. So your deductions will do you more good in 1987 rather than 1988—unless you can itemize in 1988 and cannot in 1987. (Sorry this is so complicated!)

89 REDUCE YOUR CONSUMER DEBT.

If you use credit cards, discipline yourself to pay your bills on time, so as not to incur interest charges. These charges are now unconscionably high. Watch out for cards that hit you with interest if you have any debts at all, or if you're a few days late in paying one month's debt and your next month's debt (which you haven't even been billed for) is over a certain amount.

If you use credit cards and cannot help owing interest, choose a card that charges the lowest interest rates around. A credit-union card is usually a good bet. Or use a charge card, like American Express, which normally doesn't assess interest but expects you to pay your debts promptly. Or consider a home-equity loan, because the interest you'll owe may be fully tax-deductible. (See Chapter 10.)

90 PREPAY JANUARY'S MORTGAGE IN DECEMBER . . .

if you think you can itemize this year, but you're not sure about next year. (Remember: Mortgage debt is generally deductible in full, unlike consumer debt; so, unlike consumer interest, there's no reason to speed up payments.) If your lender's yearly notice reports that you've paid one month's less interest than you're claiming on your tax return, just attach an explanation to your return—"January mortgage interest paid in December."

91 DON'T BE AFRAID OF BORROWING.

In general, borrowing is less desirable now, with interest deductions being curtailed. But 65 percent or 40 percent deductibility is still worth paying attention to. Let's say that you have $5,000 to invest in a certificate of deposit; if you invest $10,000, you'll receive a significantly higher return. So, you may be better off borrowing $5,000 (the interest on which is still partly deductible) to get the higher rate on a $10,000 investment. Work out the figures, using the different rates available and considering your tax bracket.

But, you may ask, if you borrow to buy a CD, isn't the interest you pay investment income—deductible up to your net investment income? The IRS hasn't ruled on that yet.

92 REDUCE YOUR INVESTMENT INTEREST.

Tax reform has lowered the amount of interest that you can deduct if you borrow money to invest. In 1991, you will be allowed to deduct such interest only to the extent of your net investment income—your investment income minus investment expenses (but not minus investment interest).

In the meantime, you can still deduct part of your excess investment interest. If you're married and filing jointly, the amount you use to calculate with is $10,000. Use $5,000 if you're married and filing separately.

For 1987, you can deduct 65 percent of excess investment interest, up to $10,000; in 1988, 40 percent; in 1989, 20 percent; in 1990, 10 percent; and in 1991, you cannot deduct any amount above your net investment income.

Your investment INCOME doesn't include property used in your business. And your investment INTEREST doesn't include any rental (or other "passive") activity income or loss, or any expense to obtain a stake in a passive activity. (See Chapter 9.)

Any disallowance can be carried forward to the next few years. But you'll have to abide by the shrinking amount of deductions in those years.

93 DON'T OVERLOOK ANY INTEREST EXPENSES.

You can toss into the pot

• "points" you pay when you obtain a mortgage to buy or improve a house. (Points, also called loan-origination fees, are special charges a lender socks you with to keep the interest rate down; each point equals 1 percent of the loan amount.) To be deductible all at once, you must PAY the points all at once, not pay them as you pay off your mortgage; and you must pay them separately from other charges the lender assesses you with (ask for a separate bill, and pay by a separate check).

Other rules: Your lender must usually charge these points in your area, and the number of points you were charged should also be standard. Points paid, or supposedly paid, by owners when they sell a house to someone with a Veterans Adminstration–backed loan aren't deductible.

• points you pay to refinance your mortgage. Here, you can deduct the points only over the life of the mortgage (unless bills currently in Congress succeed in making them deductible all at once). If you pay 3 points on a $100,000 loan, you wind up owing $3,000. If yours is a fifteen-year mortgage, you can deduct $200 a year. If, before the fifteen years are up, you pay off the mortgage—because you sell the house, or you just want a mortgage-free house—you can deduct the remainder of the points in the year you pay them.

• certain penalties. Let's say that you DO pay off your mortgage early. The lender may hit you with a charge of a few hundred dollars, especially if you clear up the mortgage in the first few years. This penalty, unlike most other penalties, can be deducted. Also, if your mortgage-holder assesses you an extra charge because you paid your monthly installment late, that penalty is deductible. So are penalties levied by credit-card and charge-card lenders, if the penalty is really extra interest, based on the unpaid balance, and not a fixed charge. The same goes for penalties for late payments assessed by an electric and gas company.

• interest you owe because you didn't pay all the taxes you should have. (This is considered consumer interest, even if the taxes you owed were from your business activities.)

• a portion of the interest you owe on the mortgage the cooperative owns if you're a member of the coop. Remember: Interest on a mortgage may be fully deductible.

94 DON'T BE AFRAID OF HAVING DEBTS ALONG WITH MUNIS.

The rule is that you cannot deduct interest if you use money you borrowed in order to buy tax-exempt securities, like municipal bonds, annuities, or cash-value life insurance. But that doesn't mean, for example, you can never have a mortgage and munis at the same time. There must be a direct link between the debts and the tax-exempt instruments before you are forbidden to deduct interest payments.

One woman borrowed to pay her taxes; she could deduct the interest, even though she owned municipal bonds. So could a man who borrowed money to start a business, deciding not to sell the municipals he owned. Another taxpayer borrowed money to buy a business; there was an unforeseen delay in the purchase. So he temporarily parked the money in municipal bonds—and a court approved his deducting the interest he had paid.

95 BORROW TO BUY TAX-EXEMPT INVESTMENTS . . .

and deduct the interest if the tax-exempts are only a tiny part of your portfolio. The IRS rule: The tax-exempts should constitute less than 2 percent of the average basis (cost for tax purposes) of your portfolio investments and business assets.

You can also fully deduct the interest you pay when you borrow from your insurance contracts—if the interest is $100 or less, if you have a financial emergency, or if your borrowing is related to your business.

96 BORROW FROM YOUR STOCKBROKER . . .

if you're determined to buy securities with borrowed money. His or her charges will be considered investment interest.

You cannot use the money for noninvestment purposes if you want the interest to be totally deductible. Keep in mind, though, that using your margin account to borrow stocks, Treasury obligations, or anything else is very risky, even for professional investors.

97 REPAY A DEBT BY BORROWING ONLY FROM SOMEONE ELSE.

If you owe (say) Chase Manhattan $10,000, don't borrow $12,000 from Chase to pay off your $10,000 debt. The interest you owed may not be considered deductible. Borrow the $12,000 from (say) Citibank—or from your rich uncle.

98 BORROW FROM YOUR FAMILY.

You can deduct the interest you pay if the loan was genuine—it wasn't really a gift, or you weren't charged a ridiculously low interest rate. Provide your family member (a minor child qualifies) with collateral; spell out the terms (interest rate and payment schedule) in a note. The benefit, of course, is that your family member enjoys a high rate of interest—or you enjoy a low one.

A man I know borrowed from his young son's custodial account. The father had just purchased a car, and was paying a bank 13 percent interest on the loan. He borrowed from his son, used the money to pay off the bank, and began paying the child 13 percent interest—far more than the child could have earned safely elsewhere. And the father had all of the bank's printed vouchers to guide him in repaying the loan over the next few years. While borrowing from a custodial account is considered perilous, in this case everything was so aboveboard and sensible that the man's accountant and his lawyer gave their approval.

A man's wife refused to tell him about her plans to divorce him. She agreed to tell him if he lent her money.

He conceded; she told all; the interest he paid was deductible. (Yes, it was consumer interest.) The same was true in a case where a wife lent her husband money to start a business.

99 DEDUCT A ONETIME FINANCE CHARGE . . .

for each advance your bank adds to your charge-card balance. The fees that banks have charged for this service have run from 1 percent to 2 percent of the advance.

100 DEDUCT "IMPUTED" INTEREST.

Let's say that you buy a home from someone for $100,000, and the seller gives you a mortgage at a wonderfully low interest rate—5 percent. Actually, the house is worth only $90,000. The seller is really charging you $10,000 for that 5 percent interest rate. In situations like this, you can deduct the "imputed" interest—what you're really paying. (When you sell the house and figure out your capital gains, you'll have to use a purchase price lower than that $100,000.) You may need professional help to figure out what you can deduct. Or consult IRS Publication 537, INSTALLMENT SALES.

101 DEDUCT USURIOUS INTEREST.

The IRS doesn't care that you pay an exorbitant rate of interest, a rate that infringes state usury laws.

In fact, if you innocently borrowed money from someone who embezzled the money in the first place, you're still entitled to deduct the interest.

MISCELLANEOUS DEDUCTIONS

102
DON'T SUBTRACT 2 PERCENT FROM ALL MISCELLANEOUS DEDUCTIONS.

Moving expenses, for example, aren't subject to the new floor you must surpass to deduct the assorted expenses gathered under "miscellaneous" deductions. The new floor: 2 percent of your adjusted gross income (your total income minus things like pension contributions and alimony you pay).

Other itemized deductions that bypass the new 2 percent rule:

• gambling losses—up to your income from gambling (this was meant as a favor to the many people now playing state lotteries)

• deductions for mortgage interest and real-estate taxes on a cooperative you own

• expenses of "short" sales (When you sell a stock short, you borrow the stock, then actually buy it and replace it later on, when—you hope—the price has gone down; you'll owe regular dividends to the person whose stock you borrowed, and you may have to spring for capital gains as well, if the stock's price went up.)

• wasted payments you made for an annuity that you dropped

• the work expenses of a handicapped person relating to the impairment (typically, paying an attendant to help on the job, and the cost of special tools)

• estate taxes on income you received from someone who died. This is money earned by a decedent that went to you, not subject to income tax, but where the decedent's estate paid a Federal estate tax on that income.

• certain "claims of right" you paid. Example: You reported income in a prior year, but you had to pay back that income (the payer may have successfully sued you for it, or paid you by mistake).

• certain employment expenses paid by performing artists (see Chapter 10)

• a premium you paid to buy a bond. If you paid more for a bond than its face value, your extra expense is deductible—year by year, until the bond matures or until the year you sell it. (A bond may have been selling for $1,200 a unit, when its face value was $1,000—because it originally paid an unusually high rate of interest, and you were therefore eager to buy it.)

103 DON'T FORGET ANY MISCELLANEOUS DEDUCTIONS.

Among them (and all are subject to the 2 percent of adjusted-gross-income floor):

• most unreimbursed employee business expenses, as for travel, meals, and entertainment (but deduct 20 percent from meals and entertainment costs first); the use of your home phone for business (add in the 3 percent Federal excise taxes and local sales taxes, too); education (see Chapter 11); the cost of searching for a new job in the same field you're in now; union dues and dues for a professional association (like the American Medical Association or the Chamber of Commerce); work clothes that are required but you can't normally wear outside the office, along with safety equipment like goggles and hard hats; certain costs of an office at home (see Chapter 11); subscriptions to business and trade publications you need for your job; malpractice or errors and omissions insurance; medical examinations your employer requires; employment-agency and career-counseling fees; a college professor's research, lecturing, and writing expenses.

• investment expenses. Fees charged by your investment adviser or manager, or by a trust administrator; subscriptions to publications like *Sylvia Porter's Personal Finance*

Magazine (you expect me to mention a competitor?), the *Wall Street Journal*, and this book; rental charges for a safe-deposit box if you keep taxable securities there; fees paid to a custodian of property you have that produces income; a rented office and staff needed to watch your investments; fees you pay a lawyer to collect money owed to you, and other such legal costs (like summonses and court fees); investment travel and entertainment expenses (the latter must be reduced by 20 percent first).

• tax-related expenses. What you pay someone to prepare your tax returns, or to give you tax advice about your employment contract, alimony, or divorce; appraisals to determine the amount of a casualty loss, or whatever you're contributing to charity; expenses in connection with a hobby, up to your income from that hobby.

104 DEDUCT FOR UNION DUES . . .

even if you're not a member, but you must belong to the union.

If you would be dropped from membership unless you pay a fine, the fine is deductible.

105 ASK FOR AN EXPENSE ACCOUNT.

Today, if your employer doesn't pay you directly for your expenses, you can deduct only 80 percent of unreimbursed business meal and entertainment expenses—and only that much if you itemize, and your miscellaneous expenses surpass a floor of 2 percent of your adjusted gross income.

So it's time to ask your boss to be reimbursed directly, via an expense account, and not to be expected to pay such expenses yourself, out of your salary.

106 DON'T OVERLOOK ANY SMALL TRAVEL EXPENSES . . .

such as the cost of dry cleaning and laundry, and phone calls home, as well as transportation, food, and lodgings.

Travel expenses are those you incur outside the metropolitan area where you work, if you remain overnight—or at least long enough to need some rest before you return.

107 DEDUCT FOR THE COST OF SITUATION-WANTED ADS.

Other job-hunting expenses you might overlook: phone calls to set up interviews, photocopying of documents (like articles you've written or presentations you've made), photographs that accompany your résumés, stamps and envelopes to mail out résumés, and transportation to potential employers and to employment agencies. Remember that even if you turn down a job offer, or if you're turned down, you can deduct the cost.

108 DEDUCT THE COST OF A REWARD . . .

if you lost a briefcase or other valuable business property, and you paid for an advertisement and the reward.

109 DEDUCT THE COST OF ATTENDING A STOCKHOLDERS' MEETING . . .

if you went for a specific purpose (to complain about the officers' high salaries, for example) and if your holdings in the stock are a significant part of your portfolio. Deduct travel, meals (subtract 20 percent first), and lodging.

110 DEDUCT THE EXPENSE OF VISITING YOUR STOCKBROKER . . .

if you went there for consultation, not to watch the ticker tape. The same is true if you visit an investment adviser, an accountant, or a lawyer who advises you on taxes or estate planning.

111 DEDUCT YOUR SHARE OF OPERATING EXPENSES FOR AN INVESTMENT CLUB . . .

except for expenses linked with tax-exempt income.

112 DEDUCT INSURANCE YOU BOUGHT TO COVER LOST TAXABLE SECURITIES.

If you lost a security, you won't be issued a replacement until you post an indemnity bond—in case the person who found the security cashes it in. You can deduct the cost.

113 TRY TO ITEMIZE YOUR MOVING EXPENSES.

You will lose these expenses, which can be high, if you can't itemize. That's why it's important to keep track of all your expenses, and to try to itemize in the year you move, or incur expenses for moving. Thus, if you move in 1988 and your employer isn't covering the cost, try to lower your adjusted gross income (by giving the maximum to pension plans, for example). By lowering your adjusted gross income, you're more likely to be able to take deductions with floors you must surpass—medical expenses, casualty losses, and certain miscellaneous expenses. Also try to bolster your deductions (by, for example, accelerating contributions to a charity).

Reasonable moving expenses paid by an employee or by a self-employed person in connection with his or her job are deductible—if they meet certain complicated requirements. Claim the deduction on Form 3903.

Deductible moving expenses are either (a) direct or (b) indirect. The chief difference is that there's no limit on the deduction for direct moving expenses, while there are limits on the indirect ones.

Direct expenses include:

a. the cost of moving household goods and personal effects (including crating and packing) from your old to your new residence, plus

b. you and your family's transportation expenses (including meals and lodgings) while traveling from the old to the new residence.

Indirect expenses include:

a. the cost of any round-trips (including meals and lodging) you and members of your household took mainly to find a new residence—providing that you have already obtained a new job, or (if you're self-employed) you've made "substantial" arrangements to begin working at the new location;

b. the cost of meals and lodging for you and members of your family during the thirty consecutive days after you get your new job and while you're staying in temporary quarters (whether you're still looking for a new residence, or waiting to move in);

c. the cost of selling and buying a new residence, or terminating an old lease, including lawyers' fees, escrow fees, appraisal fees, real-estate agent's commissions, "points" (a special fee for a mortgage), and title-insurance costs. (If you can't itemize, add some of these to the basis—

cost, for tax purposes—of your new residence, or to the sales price of your old residence, so you'll reduce your eventual capital gains.)

You can deduct DIRECT moving expenses only if

a. you move to a new main job that's at least thirty-five miles farther away from your old residence than the old job was (subtract the distance in miles from your old residence to your old job, then subtract that number from the distance from your old residence to your new job, and hope that you get at least thirty-five); and

b. during the twelve months after you're at your new job, you're a full-time employee for at least thirty-nine weeks—or, if self-employed, you work full-time for at least seventy-eight weeks during the twenty-four months after you arrive at the new location. Exceptions to these thirty-nine-week and seventy-eight-week requirements are listed below.

You can deduct INDIRECT moving expenses only if they meet the requirements listed above for DIRECT moving expenses. The amounts you can deduct for INDIRECT expenses are

a. no more than $1,500 for trips to find a new house before moving, and for temporary living expenses at your new job; and

b. no more than $3,000 for the expenses of selling, buying, or renting a residence, minus the amount you're allowed under (a).

114 CONSIDER WAITING BEFORE SEEKING A NEW RESIDENCE.

To deduct your moving expenses, you have a year to move after you start a new job. So if you begin your job late in the year, you might wait until the next year before moving—

if you think that the next year you'll be able to itemize, but this year you can't. You'll have to balance your possible deductions against the cost of a temporary residence, as well as the deprivation of possibly not having your family with you.

115 YOU CAN MOVE FARTHER AWAY FROM YOUR NEW JOB IF . . .

your new residence is much more convenient to your new place of work. For example, at your new residence you may have better public transportation, or you can drive on a highway to your office, not back roads.

116 YOU CAN CHANGE JOBS IN YOUR NEW AREA . . .

and still meet the thirty-nine-week test, so long as you remain in the same general area. And you can even take some time off during those twelve months after you start a new job, because the thirty-nine weeks don't have to be consecutive.

117 YOU CAN FAIL THE TIME TEST . . .

and still deduct moving expenses, if you're in the armed forces and moved because you were permanently transferred, or you moved to the U.S.A. because you retired, or you're laid off for reasons other than "willful misconduct." The IRS states: "The time test also does not have to be met in the case of death."

118 DEDUCT MOVING EXPENSES EVEN IF YOU'VE NEVER WORKED BEFORE.

A student (for example) starting a first job can deduct moving expenses, providing that the student moved from a former main residence to a new one. (A college dorm isn't a main residence.) The same goes for people entering the job market after a long period of unemployment—like a homemaker.

119 IF YOU HAVE A LOSS ON SELLING YOUR HOME . . .

you can't deduct it. So try to deduct a real-estates agent's commission as a moving expense, not as an expense of selling your home. What if you have a gain on your sale? If you've also reached the $1,500 limit on house-hunting and temporary living expenses, and the limit of $1,500 on home sales expenses WITHOUT the sales commission, use the commission to reduce the gain on the sale of your house— to lower your possible capital-gains taxes.

120 RENTERS CAN DEDUCT LEGAL FEES . . .

to extricate themselves from a lease; for payments to their landlords for releasing them from a lease; for real-estate agent's fees; for the difference between the rent they pay now if it's higher than the rent they receive from the person who took over their residence; and for the cost of finding a replacement tenant. In renting a new residence, you can also deduct legal fees and the fees of a real-estate agent.

121 DEDUCT A LOST SECURITY DEPOSIT.

If you were renting and lost your security deposit because you broke your lease, it's deductible—but not if you lost the deposit because of damage to the residence.

122 DON'T CURTAIL HOUSE-HUNTING TRIPS.

There's no limit on the trips you can take, and still deduct the expense, once you have a new job.

123 DON'T DEDUCT JUST 9 CENTS A MILE IF YOU USE YOUR CAR.

You're probably better off keeping a record of your actual expenses for oil and gas, parking fees, and tolls.

124 DON'T GIVE UP IF YOU DIDN'T MOVE TO YOUR NEW AREA IN A YEAR.

If you had a good reason for your delay, you may be excused—and your moving expenses will remain deductible. Example: You wanted your daughter to graduate from her old high school. (But, oddly enough, not having sold your old house yet isn't an acceptable excuse.)

125 DEDUCT FOR MOVING BACK TO THE U.S.A. . . .

if you retire while working or living overseas, or if you are the survivor (spouse or dependent) of someone who died while working overseas. (See Chapter 11 for other deductible expenses for employees.)

Chapter Four
MEDICAL EXPENSES

Tax reform made few changes with regard to your deducting medical expenses on Schedule A. But one of those changes was a beaut.

Now, if you itemize all your deductions, the only medical and dental expenses you can actually write off are those that exceed 7.5 percent of your adjusted gross income (your total income minus things like contributions to IRAs). The old percentage was 5 percent. This means that you must have very large medical expenses before you can deduct anything. If your adjusted gross income is $30,000, you must have $2,250 in medical expenses before you can start deducting anything.

What can you do? Push or pull medical expenses into a year when you think (a) you'll be able to itemize, and (b) you'll have unusually large medical expenses. In other words,

126 BUNCH YOUR DEDUCTIONS.

One way is to pay your bills either this year, or next—assuming that your bills arrive near the end of the year. If you're strapped for cash, you can pay your bills by credit card this year, and take deductions this year, while paying the credit-card company next year. (If you would incur high credit-card interest, forget it. Just delay your payments.)

You can also postpone some of your sessions with health-care people. Perhaps a few of your possible expenditures are "elective"—you needn't have them done immediately. You can have your teeth capped this year or next. Or get bifocals* this year or the following one. Or postpone a gallbladder operation if your doctor says, "It should come out one of these days." Or defer surgery that's just to improve your appearance. Of course, don't postpone any medical or dental care you really need, just to save on your taxes.

Another way to push your expenses into another year is to defer filing for health-insurance coverage. Let's say that you have an appendectomy late in the year. You might file for coverage in December, knowing that you won't receive payment until January. When you receive your payment, you'll declare it as income in that year—instead of subtracting it from your medical expenses the previous year.

If you decide to try pushing health expenses into, say, 1989, also try to speed up expenses you'd normally incur in 1990 into 1989. Get your physical early. See your dentist a little sooner. And pay your bills in 1989—even if your doctors or dentists haven't sent them (because they're practicing "bunching," too).

What if you expect to surpass the 7.5 percent floor in two consecutive years? Push your medical expenses into the year in which you may have a higher income—because you might be in a higher tax bracket, and deductions will save you more money.

If you're reading this in 1987, you should probably try to nail down all your deductions in 1987—because your tax bracket will probably be lower next year (the top tax rate is going from 38.5 percent to 33 percent or 28 percent).

If it's impossible for you to decide in which year your medical expenses may exceed 7.5 percent of your adjusted gross income, try to make your expenditures early in any current year. You'll have the remainder of the year to add to them. And it's almost always better to obtain deductions as soon as possible—so you'll have more income sooner.

If you want to claim your deductions this year and don't have enough money to pay your bills, consider a home-equity loan. The interest you pay on loans for medical expenses—even against the appreciation of your house—is totally tax-deductible. (See Chapter 10.) Personal interest you pay is only 65 percent deductible in 1987, 40 percent in 1988.

127 REMEMBER THAT THERE'S NO TOP LIMIT ON MEDICAL EXPENSES.

While there's a floor (7.5 percent of your adjusted gross income), there's no ceiling. You can deduct all your medical–dental expenses to the point where you owe no taxes at all.

128 INCLUDE MORE THAN YOUR OWN EXPENSES.

You can include, of course, your own expenses and those of your spouse if you file a joint return, as well as bills you paid for

a. all dependents you list on your return,

b. any person (like a child or parent) you COULD have listed on your return as a dependent IF that person didn't have $1,900 or more in income (for 1987) or $1,950 (for 1988), and didn't file a joint return with his or her spouse. Example: You contributed more than half your mother's support, but you cannot claim her as a dependent because she had $1,900 in gross income during 1987. Yet you can include any of her medical expenses that you yourself paid as your own medical expenses.

Who else's expenses can you include? The surgical, hospital, laboratory, and transportation expenses of someone who came to your hospital to provide you with a body organ—for example, a kidney.

Another possibility: You can pay and deduct the medical expenses of a child you've made arrangements to adopt— even if the child isn't born yet! The child must have qualified as your dependent when the medical services were furnished, or when you actually paid them.

129 DEDUCT MEDICAL EXPENSES YOU PAID FOR A NONDEPENDENT CHILD . . .

if you were divorced under a decree after 1984. You can't deduct such medical expenses if you were divorced under an earlier agreement.

130 CONSIDER PAYING YOUR PARENTS' MEDICAL BILLS.

If they have relatively low taxes and relatively high medical bills, think about paying their medical expenses. If your payments of their medical bills, plus other support you give them, add up to over half their total support for the year, you may reap three tax advantages: (a) you can deduct the medical expenses you pay, (b) you may be able to claim them as dependents on your own tax return, and (c) if you're not married, you may be able to use the lower head-of-household tax rates in figuring what you owe.

131 DEDUCT THIS YEAR FOR LIFETIME CARE.

If you paid a lump sum for a dependent's or spouse's lifetime care in a retirement home, or the lifetime care of a handicapped child, you can deduct the cost in the year you made the payment. But in general, for medical expenses to be deductible, you cannot pay them in advance.

132 INCLUDE THE COST OF PRESCRIPTION MEDICINES AND INSULIN.

Keep your receipts. Or consider patronizing a pharmacy that will send you a report on all your prescription purchases for the year; many pharmacies are happy to oblige.

You cannot deduct the cost of drugs unless prescribed by a physician. If your doctor tells you to take two aspirin and call him/her in the morning, deduct the bill he/she sends you and the cost of the phone call—but not the aspirin, which isn't a prescription drug.

133 INCLUDE THE COST OF INSURANCE YOU PAY FOR.

Not just health insurance ("basic" or "first dollar," as well as major medical), but dental insurance, "catastrophic" insurance (special policies that give you a maximum coverage of perhaps $1 million), disability insurance, and Medicare. Also include the cost of belonging to a health-maintenance organization.

If you employer charges you for group coverage, your payments are deductible. Many employers don't inform their employees, at the end of the year, how much the employees have paid for health insurance. Either ask for an accounting, or keep your paycheck stubs and add up the totals.

Don't forget to include payments for Social Security Medical B insurance (supplementary health insurance for the aged). The premiums are either deducted from your monthly benefit check, or you pay them directly.

Insurance you buy for accidental death, or loss of limbs, doesn't qualify. Nor does the cost of insurance that pays you a flat amount per week or month while you're ill or not working—because that insurance doesn't necessarily cover medical expenses. And skip the insurance you pay for the medical expenses of anyone injured in your car or by your car, or in your house.

Of course, any deductions you claim must first be reduced by reimbursements you received for medical–dental expenses. But you need not reduce your expenses by payments you've received for personal injuries, or for loss of your earnings, or the flat fees that a policy pays you if you're ill and out of work.

134 DON'T OVERLOOK ANY OTHER INSURANCE YOU PAY.

Does your school charge you for insurance in case your child is injured in sports? Does your child's summer camp? The premiums are deductible. So is the cost of insuring your contact lenses against loss or damage.

135 DEDUCT 25 PERCENT OF YOUR MEDICAL EXPENSES DIRECTLY FROM GROSS INCOME . . .

if (a) you're self-employed (the remaining 75 percent is an itemized deduction, subject to the 7.5 percent floor); (b) your health-insurance plan also covers your employees; (c) your deduction doesn't exceed your income from self-employment; and (d) you're NOT also employed by someone else, and don't have the option of joining your employer's plan, or the plan of your spouse's employer, at a reduced rate.

This special break is to give the self-employed a benefit like the one enjoyed by employees who receive health insurance free of charge.

But this concession applies only to tax returns for years after 1986 and BEFORE 1990. It might expire in 1990.

136 KEEP YOUR GAIN IF YOU HAD EXCESS INSURANCE COVERAGE.

Let's say that your hospital stay cost you $600, and two insurance policies paid you a total of $800. If you actually paid the premiums on the policies—your employer didn't pay either one—you need not declare or pay taxes on the gains you made. If some of your insurance was paid by you, some by your employer, you'll have to apportion your profit.

If you're reimbursed in the year after you had medical expenses, report the payments as income in the year you received them. But don't report more than any amount you previously deducted as a medical expense. If you didn't claim any deduction for these medical expenses—because you didn't itemize, or you didn't surpass the floor—again, you needn't report the reimbursement as income.

137 INCLUDE THE COST OF TRANSPORTATION.

Figure in the cost of cab fare, buses, trains, planes, or your driving to a doctor's office, hospital, pharmacy, or to a laboratory. You can either calculate the expense at 9 cents a mile, or tote up the real costs (if you drive, your mileage times what you pay for gas, plus any oil your car needs). Don't deduct for car depreciation, repairs, maintenance, or car insurance. Whether you use the 9-cents-a-mile approach, or the actual cost, throw in whatever you paid for tolls and parking.

You can also deduct the cost of a nurse's traveling expenses if he/she accompanies you to a clinic, and gives you care you need (like medications or injections) during the trip.

A women with a rare skin disease went to Europe to be treated by a doctor knowledgeable about her disease. She could deduct her travel costs along with his fees.

A man traveling to Europe on a freighter for a vacation

had a recurrence of a severe kidney disorder. He flew back to San Francisco for emergency treatment by his urologist, and deducted the higher cost of the plane trip.

138 ADD THE COST OF HOTELS . . .

or other lodgings if you traveled somewhere mainly to be cared for by a physician in a licensed hospital or similar health-care facility. The cost of the lodgings cannot be more than $50 a night for the patient and for another eligible person, like a parent accompanying a dependent child. In other words, two people can spend $100. Be careful not to claim the cost of a luxury motel, or spend much of your time there sight-seeing or vacationing.

139 DEDUCT THE COST OF A TRIP TO A WARMER CLIMATE . . .

if a physician prescribes it to help a chronic ailment you (or your spouse or dependent) has, like asthma. But you can't deduct the cost of meals and lodgings on your visit unless you stay in a hospital. And you cannot deduct the cost of a trip to a weight-reduction spa, or for the improvement of your general physical or mental health.

140 DON'T FORGET A VARIETY OF OTHER EXPENSES.

Such as the cost of

- ambulance service
- phone calls to doctors, nurses, hospitals, insurers, and so forth
- artificial limbs, braces, elastic stockings, canes, crutches, wheelchairs, orthopedic shoes (beyond the cost of normal shoes), eyeglasses, medically needed whirlpools

- fluoridating devices recommended by a dentist
- blood-sugar tests
- guide dogs (for the blind or deaf), along with their care and feeding
- books and magazines in Braille (above the cost of ordinary versions)
- special telephone equipment for the deaf, along with repairs
- hearing aids and their maintenance (including batteries)
- special foods or drinks solely for the treatment of an illness (like the cost of whiskey for a heart patient)
- special instruction in lip reading and speech for a deaf person
- special therapy for someone recovering from a stroke
- removal of lead-based paint from the walls of a house in which a child contracted lead poisoning from eating such paint. (Either the area must be within the child's reach, or the paint must be peeling or cracking, and thus likely to fall.)
- a special mattress and headboard if you have arthritis.

Also include the extra cost of

- a TV set, or an adapter for an existing set, to provide subtitles for someone who's deaf;
- a car designed to accommodate a wheelchair, or special controls in a car for the handicapped.

Here are other real cases, just to prompt you to consider other possible expenses:

An orthodontist recommended clarinet lessons for a boy with severe malocclusion. The cost of the clarinet, along with the lessons, was deductible.

A man was placed on a strict salt-free diet. He was allowed to deduct the extra fees that restaurants charged him for preparing salt-free food, as well as his expenses traveling to and from these restaurants.

A woman who made her living donating blood was permitted to deduct the cost of high-protein food and vitamin supplements.

A woman worked as a clerk in her husband's store. Her mother needed home care, and the woman agreed to help her—on the condition that her brother pay another clerk to replace her in the store. The brother agreed, and deducted the store clerk's salary as a medical expense on his own return.

A man deducted the legal fees he paid to obtain guardianship over a relative who had refused psychiatric treatment.

A woman had to move to a larger apartment to accommodate a new nurse, and deducted the extra rent she had to pay.

141 DEDUCT SOCIAL SECURITY TAXES . . .

you may have to pay on the wages of a nurse or attendant whom you hired directly.

142 DEDUCT THE COST OF COSMETIC WORK.

You can include the cost of hair transplants performed by a surgeon or a dermatologist, or a face-lift (even if a physician didn't recommend it), or having excess hair removed via electrolysis by a state-licensed technician.

A woman who had lost her hair was allowed to deduct the cost of a wig that her doctor recommended to prevent her from becoming depressed.

No, the cost of having your ears pierced or getting tattooed doesn't qualify.

143 WRITE OFF THE COST OF PRESCRIBED BIRTH-CONTROL DEVICES.

Examples: birth-control pills, a diaphragm bought by prescription, a vasectomy, female sterilization, an abortion.

144 DEDUCT FOR AIR-CONDITIONING WHEN YOU HAVE AN ALLERGY . . .

if (a) your doctor prescribed it mainly to relieve your breathing, and gives you a statement saying so; and (b) the air conditioner is detachable—it isn't built into the wall of the house (that would turn it into an improvement that boosts the value of your house). You're supposed to deduct whatever salvage value you think the air conditioner may eventually have—what you might sell it for.

If you buy a vacuum cleaner to remove dust from your residence, to deduct the cost you would again need a physician's recommendation, as well as evidence that you wouldn't have bought it except for your allergy. (You might argue that you already had a carpet sweeper that did all the cleaning needed.)

145 DEDUCT THE COST OF A DRUG-TREATMENT CENTER.

Treatment at a center for alcoholics also qualifies. But not, oddly enough, treatment at a center that helps people stop smoking.

146 DEDUCT THE COST OF A WEIGHT-REDUCTION PROGRAM . . .

if a physician prescribed it NOT just because you're a little overweight, but because of a specific medical condition you have—like a heart problem compounded by your excess weight, or even for obesity (being grossly overweight).

147 WRITE OFF THE COST OF A SWIMMING POOL...

if it was recommended by your physician, and if you first subtract the amount that such a permanent improvement added to the value of your house. (If it's a removable aboveground pool, deduct the salvage value.) Thus, if the pool cost $20,000, and adds $5,000 to your house, your deduction is $15,000. (Swimming pools rarely add much to a house's value unless you live in a state where the weather tends to be warm year-round.)

To demonstrate that a pool was installed for health reasons, you would be wise to buy a low-cost and not a luxury model. And skip a diving board or slide.

One couple was able to deduct their pool by arguing that they never entertained people there. But another couple wasn't allowed much of a deduction, even though a doctor had recommended a pool for the wife's spinal condition. The pool was oversized, built with hand-cut stone and cedar woodwork, in a building with a cathedral ceiling.

If your new pool is indoors, you can deduct the percentage of your home-heating costs that warm the room it's in.

The same guidelines apply to most other medically related home improvements—permanent air conditioners, central air-conditioning, home elevators or inclinators, and bedrooms and bathrooms added to a lower floor so that a patient doesn't have to do much stair-climbing. (For exceptions, see Tip 150.)

First deduct the amount that the improvements add to the value of the house. (Many real-estate agents can do such appraisals.) And don't buy the top-of-the-line model, or your deduction may be limited to what a moderately priced improvement would have cost you.

148 DEDUCT FOR QUASI-HOSPITAL ROOMS.

A man rented a two-room apartment in his building for his mother, who, her physician had advised, needed extended care after being hospitalized. The son engaged a full-time nurse, and furnished the rooms with medical equipment. He was allowed a full deduction for the rent because the rooms were similar to what a hospital or extended-care facility would have provided.

In a similar case, a man wasn't allowed to remain in his hospital room after an appendectomy. So he checked into a nearby hotel until he recovered. His wife changed his bandages and helped him get around. The hotel's cost was deductible: It was regarded as a substitute for a hospital room.

149 DON'T FORGET OPERATING EXPENSES.

The electricity that runs the air conditioner for your allergy, and the cost of having it repaired and maintained, are deductible. The same goes for other doctor-recommended devices, like the cost of maintaining and running an elevator for a heart patient, or a special bath for an arthritis patient.

150 DON'T SUBTRACT THE VALUE OF CERTAIN IMPROVEMENTS.

Thanks to tax reform, you can now deduct the full cost (above the floor of 7.5 percent of your adjusted gross income) of removing structural barriers in a personal residence to make life easier for a handicapped person.

Thus, the following expenditures do NOT add to the value of a residence, for tax purposes: (a) constructing entrance or exit ramps; (b) widening doorways; (c) modifying interior doorways and hallways to accommodate wheelchairs; (d) installing railings and support bars in bathrooms, along with similar changes; (e) lowering kitchen cabinets and other equipment to make it easier for the handicapped to reach them; (f) adjustments of electrical outlets and fixtures.

151 DEDUCT THE COST OF AN OLD-AGE HOME FOR YOUR PARENT . . .

to the extent that your money goes for nursing or medical care. Ask the home to provide you with a breakdown of the charges. If your parent is in the home mainly for medical reasons, you can even deduct the cost of meals and lodgings.

152 DEDUCT THE COST OF A SPECIAL SCHOOL FOR A HANDICAPPED CHILD.

Examples: A blind child attends a school to learn Braille, a deaf child to learn lip-reading, a retarded child to receive special instruction. (While such a school may provide some normal educational classes, this cannot be the school's main purpose.)

Similarly, you can deduct the cost of remedial-reading courses if a child is brain-damaged, and the cost of a halfway house (including room and board) for a patient making a transition from a mental hospital to life in the community.

If your visits to and from the school are considered necessary for the child's therapy, your travel expenses are deductible.

153 DEDUCT PART OF THE COST OF HOUSEHOLD HELP FOR A SEMI-INVALID.

Divvy up the wages you paid between deductible medical care and nondeductible personal services, like house-cleaning. (One court let a woman deduct 75 percent of the expenses, without apportioning them.)

154 HIRE YOUR RELATIVES.

You can have them care for an invalid, pay them, and deduct whatever percentage was purely medical. This is generally true even if your relatives have no medical or nursing training. If someone not licensed as a nurse provides nursing services, the cost is deductible.

If a relative, or a regular nurse, cares for someone in your home, deduct the cost of meals you provide, along with any wages you pay.

155 DON'T OVERLOOK THE FEES OF UNUSUAL THERAPISTS.

You can, of course, deduct fees paid to medical doctors and osteopathic physicians, dentists, nurses, and psychologists. But you can also write off the fees of nonmedical doctors like

- acupuncturists
- chiropodists (podiatrists)
- chiropractors
- Christian Science practitioners
- optometrists
- unlicensed psychotherapists

Parents were allowed to deduct fees paid to a teacher trained to deal with dyslexic children. The reading disorder, in this case, was caused by brain damage; it might not have been deductible otherwise.

The experience, qualifications, and title of the therapist don't matter. What matters: that the services rendered are medically required.

In a case where an osteopath was treating a patient by manipulation, payments the patient also made to masseurs were deductible. And—are you ready for this?—payments by a Navajo Indian to tribal medical men for healing ceremonies were allowed.

The cost of dubious medications, like laetrile, is deductible if prescribed by a physician and purchased and used in an area where the sale and use are legal.

If you or your spouse had very high medical or dental bills, consider filing separately. Figure it out both ways, separately and joint. Should one spouse have enormous bills, he or she may be able to surpass the floor of 7.5 percent of your adjusted gross income—and reduce the total taxes you must pay.

Chapter Five
CASUALTY AND THEFT LOSSES

Tax reform left deductions for casualties and thefts pretty much alone. One important change: you must file for insurance reimbursement (or estimate your insurance reimbursement) before you can take any deductions.

The old rules remain as complicated as ever.

The amount of your casualty loss is the LESSER of

a. the drop in the fair market value of your property, or

b. the cost of your investment in the property (your "basis").

Let's say that a burglar made off with your jewelry. It was worth $5,000; of course, it's valueless to you now. Loss: $5,000. But if you had paid only $4,000 for the jewelry a few years ago, $4,000 is your loss.

There are two reductions you must make before you can write off personal casualty losses:

1. subtract $100 from each separate occurrence (fires at different times, for example), then

2. subtract 10 percent of your adjusted gross income

(your total reportable income minus things like IRA contributions) from your remaining casualty losses.

You must deduct insurance payments or other reimbursements you receive, or MAY receive, from the value of any loss. Tax reform, as mentioned, requires that you file for insurance coverage before claiming casualty losses on your tax return—even if you're worried that reporting an accident to your insurance company may raise your premiums, or provoke the insurer to stop covering you.

Here's an example of how to calculate your deductible loss:

You bought a house for $25,000. Fifteen years later, it was worth $100,000. After a fire, it was worth only $50,000. An insurance company paid you $5,000 (unrealistic, but we need a low figure for our calculations). Your adjusted gross income is $32,500.

Value before fire: $100,000.

Value after fire: $50,000.

Decline in value: $50,000.

But remember that you're limited to the original cost of your house—$25,000. So forget about the $50,000.

If the insurance company had paid you $25,000 or more, our calculations would stop there. That's why we're using $5,000.

Subtract $5,000 from your $25,000 loss ($20,000); then subtract $100 ($19,900); then subtract 10 percent of your adjusted gross income (10 percent times $32,500 = $3,250), and you wind up with $16,650. This is your deductible loss—if you itemize, and if you have no other deductible losses that you can add to the kitty.

Our first piece of advice:

156 DON'T THINK OF JUST FIRES AND STORMS.

You may also be able to deduct losses for

• damage to your car

- theft or embezzlement
- cave-in damage on your property
- vandalism
- a burst hot-water boiler
- frozen water pipes
- earthquake damage
- damage inflicted by the pressure of ice, damage to a business establishment (such as cracking of walls and ceilings) caused by shrinkage of subsoil in a drought
- damage resulting from nearby blasting in a quarry
- damage to a septic tank caused by accidental plowing in the area

And let's not overlook losses from volcanic eruptions, shipwrecks, and sonic booms.

In general, the law won't let you take deductions for assets you've lost or mislaid, for the drop in a house's value because of threatened future flooding, or for termite damage. To qualify, the losses you suffer must be the result of a SUDDEN, UNEXPECTED, or UNUSUAL force.

A good example: A farmer was dynamiting some tree stumps on his property. His dog playfully retrieved a stick and deposited it under the farmer's car. The loss of the car was sudden, unexpected, and unusual. He could deduct the value of the car, or his cost, whichever was lower.

Another typical loss: A homeowner was having his porch turned into an enclosed den. The contractor told him that the bushes around the porch had to be cut back, so he could work unimpeded. The homeowner cut the bushes, which promptly died. The cost of identical bushes was deductible.

Other losses that have been permitted: the value of honeybees destroyed by pesticide . . . the accidental poisoning of cattle . . . the death of a horse that had eaten the lining of a hat . . . replacing sand washed away from a private beach by an unusually severe storm . . . money you've been swindled out of (if your state law considers it theft) . . . ransom money for someone who's been kidnapped.

In one memorable case, a wife left home; while she was gone, her husband gave some of her belongings to his girl friend. The wife, a court rules, was entitled to a theft–loss deduction.

157 DON'T APPLY THE REDUCTIONS TO BUSINESS LOSSES.

The $100 and 10 percent of adjusted-gross-income reductions don't hurt you if your loss was to business or income-producing property. Examples: fire damage to a room in your house you rent out, or use as an office; the theft from your factory of a photocopying machine. And with business items that are completely destroyed, or stolen, your deduction is your basis—even if your basis was MORE than the decline in the property's fair market value. (This is a special break businesspeople get.) But remember that your basis may have been reduced by depreciation, or by your taking the Section 179 expense election and writing off 10 percent of the cost in the first year. (See Chapter 12.)

158 DEDUCT LOSSES EVEN IF YOU'RE NOT THE OWNER.

If you're legally responsible for making good any loss, you can deduct the cost. Example: A tenant may be required to return rented premises to the condition in which they were originally—and thus be responsible for a fire loss. He or she can deduct the cost, subject to the usual reductions.

159 DON'T DEDUCT $100 FOR EACH DAMAGED ITEM.

If a fire destroys furniture, clothing, carpets, appliances, and books, the $100 reduction applies to all of them together, not separately. It's a $100 reduction per CASUALTY.

160 DEDUCT WHICHEVER IS GREATER—THE COST OF REPAIRS OR THE DECLINE IN VALUE.

Your car cost you $8,000. A few years later, it was worth $5,000. After an accident, its value plummeted to $2,000. Obviously, you must choose the lower loss—not your basis, but the decline in the car's value, $3,000. But what if the repairs cost more than the decline in value—$3,500? You can deduct the higher cost of the repair than the lower cost of the drop in the car's value.

161 DON'T CLAIM THE VALUE OF CHEAP REPLACEMENTS.

If your Tiffany lamp was shattered by a windstorm, don't deduct the cost of a replacement you buy at a garage sale. Deduct the cost of the lamp, or its market value. By the same token, if you're replacing plants, bushes, or trees, deduct for the mature versions—not for the cheaper seeds or saplings you may have purchased.

162 DON'T BE QUICK TO ACCEPT AN INSURANCE SETTLEMENT.

A fire destroys your living room furniture. You figure the loss at $5,000, but your insurance company, predictably, sets the loss at less—only $3,000, perhaps. If you accept the $3,000, you probably won't be able to deduct the remaining $2,000 as a casualty loss. The insurance company probably will ask that you sign a paper acknowledging that the furniture's value was $3,000. Unless $3,000 was the limit of your coverage, or you can come up with new evidence proving the furniture's value, you'll probably lose the remaining $2,000. Lesson: Give your insurer a hard time.

163   DEDUCT FOR LOSING MONEY IN A FINANCIAL INSTITUTION.

If you had money socked away in a commercial bank, savings and loan, or insured credit union that went bankrupt or became insolvent, thanks to tax reform you can now take a casualty loss—instead of a bad-debt loss. (But not if you were an officer of the troubled bank, or owned 1 percent or more of the value of the institution's stock.) Claim the loss in the year when it becomes clear that you will never get your money back.

If you deduct such a loss as a nonbusiness bad debt, it's considered a short-term loss, and you must use the loss to offset capital gains—or deduct up to $3,000 a year from your ordinary income. You may be better off taking it as a casualty loss, to get a larger deduction faster.

You can take a deduction for such financial losses as far back as 1983, if you file amended returns.

164   DEDUCT CLEANUP EXPENSES, TOO.

Usually you can add these costs to your casualty losses—the cost of removing dead trees, for example.

165   DON'T FORGET THAT THERE ARE ALWAYS EXCEPTIONS.

A drop in the value of a house because of nearby flooding is GENERALLY not deductible. But a family was allowed a $12,000 loss for the decline in their home's value when the city decided to demolish nearby houses after a flood. The destruction of the other houses apparently was a key factor—their house had become something of an orphan.

Usually a person cannot claim a casualty loss if he/she was grossly careless—crashing a car while drunk, for example, or accidentally throwing an envelope with money into a fireplace. But when a husband slammed a car door onto his wife's hand, smashing her ring, the damage to the ring was accepted as a casualty loss. Ditto the case of the husband who emptied a glass of ammonia down the garbage-disposal unit, unaware that his wife's diamond ring was rinsing in the glass. Fire damage in a house was deductible, even though the fire department blamed the blaze on a careless cook. So was the loss of a lawn when the owner applied too much weed killer. And the damage to a car resulting from the owner's having misjudged the space available in his garage. And damage to cars even though one man drove with bald tires, another with worn brake linings. Also deductible: A driver parked his car on an icy lake, and—well, you can guess.

But remember the general rule: You cannot be grossly careless and get away with deducting a casualty loss. Recently a man in Baltimore set some of his wife's clothes afire in his stove. He was a little annoyed at her—she wouldn't move to South Carolina with him, and apparently had been carrying on with another man. After setting the clothes on fire, the husband tried to quench the flames with pots of water. But the fire spread, and the entire house was destroyed.

The insurer refused to cover the damage. And when the man tried to deduct $97,900 as a casualty loss, the IRA balked. A tax court sided with the IRS: "We refuse to encourage couples to settle their disputes with fire."

Mysterious disappearances of valuable property aren't usually deductible, but the loss of a diamond from a special ring setting was accepted after a jeweler testified that it must have happened as the result of a sharp blow.

Usually damage done by insects isn't deductible. But pine beetles can wreak havoc quickly—and if they do their dirty work within around ten days, the IRS will accept such a casualty. Even termite damage has sometimes been held to be deductible. In one case, a builder and an architect testified that they had found no evidence of termites twelve months before the damage became apparent—so the termites must have been fast workers. In a similar case, the time period was fourteen months. (Such termites are sarcastically called "fast" termites.)

Droughts, like insects, tend to do damage gradually, and gradual losses usually don't qualify. But where trees died within a few months because of an unusual drought, the loss was permitted. A deduction was also allowed for damage to a home caused by a severe one-day smog. Damage to property caused by a freeze was permitted simply because it was unusual: It occurred in Florida.

In short, general rules often have exceptions. If yours is an unusual case, don't be too quick to decide you're not entitled to a casualty loss.

166 DON'T FEEL BOUND BY A CAR'S "BLUE BOOK" VALUE.

The "Blue Book" is a popular commercial guide to auto prices. But if you can prove that your damaged car was worth more than the value listed, you can deduct a higher amount. Evidence you can provide: prices for similar cars being advertised for sale in your area.

167 DON'T INCLUDE EVERY BENEFIT AS A REIMBURSEMENT.

If your house burned down and a local agency provided you with free food, lodging, and clothing, you don't have to treat them as a form of reimbursement, and need not deduct them from your loss.

168 CALL THE COPS.

What's to prevent someone from hocking jewelry, then claiming it was stolen? Having to deal with the police may be one deterrent. That's why the IRS will be less skeptical if you've notified the police after you were the victim of a theft—and you've enclosed a copy of the police report with your tax return.

In fact, you're always wise to keep evidence supporting your casualty losses, such as newspaper reports about a storm, or bills showing what you paid for the painting needed after a flood. Photographs showing the extent of a casualty loss—after a storm, for example—will also bolster your case.

Yet sometimes you can deduct a theft loss even if you didn't notify the police. These cases have passed the IRS's scrutiny: A teacher didn't report a break-in because, he explained, he suspected that students of his were the culprits, and didn't want to get them into serious trouble. A man declined to prosecute a friend who had stolen something from him after his lawyer advised that court costs would be more than the value of the missing property.

If you've lost cash, how do you prove it? One man claimed that an envelope with $36,000 had been taken from his unlocked car. Fortunately, his secretary testified that she had seen him put $36,000 into an envelope to make a down payment on some real estate he was buying. A tax court believed them.

169 CHANGE THE YEAR WHEN YOU DEDUCT YOUR LOSS.

You can do this only in one case: You live in an area that the Federal government declares a disaster area. You can then deduct your loss either in the year the disaster occurred, or during the previous year by amending your return for that year. Amending your return might get you an immediate refund; then again, you might be better off waiting until next year if you're sure you can itemize, and if your tax bracket is going up.

170 DON'T ALWAYS DEDUCT 10 PERCENT OF YOUR ADJUSTED GROSS INCOME.

Sometimes you can make a profit on a casualty loss. Let's say you bought some antique bottles for $500, and their value soared to $5,000. Then your dog knocked all of them off a shelf. Your insurance company paid you $5,000 for the loss of the bottles. You must declare the profit you've made, $4,500, as a capital gain. But if you have other casualty losses, you can deduct them from that profit.

If you're tallying together your casualty gains and your casualty losses, and your profits are greater, skip the 10 percent reduction (but not the $100 reduction) on the losses. If losses exceed gains, though, the 10 percent rules goes back into effect.

171 TRY TO AVOID BEING TAXED ON A PROFIT.

Your autograph collection cost you $5,000. When it was stolen, it was worth $10,000. Your insurance company paid you $8,000. You may have to pay taxes on the $3,000 gain—just as if you had sold the collection for $8,000. But you can get around this if you replace or repair missing or damaged property within a specified time: beginning on the day of the loss and ending two years after the end of the tax year in which you were reimbursed. (You lost your autographs in January, 1987; your insurance company reimbursed you in November, 1987; you have until December, 1989, to amass an autograph collection of similar value.)

You need not report a gain if you're reimbursed with property similar to what was destroyed—even if its value exceeded your basis. Example: Your local moving company replaces your missing furniture with more valuable furniture.

172 DEDUCT APPRAISAL FEES, EVEN IF YOU CAN'T DEDUCT A CASUALTY LOSS.

List any fee you paid an appraiser—to establish your casualty-loss deduction—as a miscellaneous expense, not subject to the $100/10 percent of adjusted-gross-income reductions. But let's hope that your other miscellaneous deductions put you over the floor of 2 percent of adjusted gross income for such expenses.

What if you pay an appraiser, then determine that you can't deduct a dime for casualty losses—because they didn't exceed 10 percent of your adjusted gross income? You're nonetheless allowed to deduct the cost as miscellaneous expense (above 2 percent of your adjusted gross income).

173 REMEMBER THAT FLORA HAVE VALUE.

You may not have paid extra for the trees, bushes, and plants on your property when you bought them, but they contributed to the value of your house. And it doesn't matter that you don't know their original cost. Find out what the property was worth before you lost any trees or shrubs, and afterward. The difference is your loss.

174 DON'T WAIT TO CLAIM A LOSS.

You can't afford to replace your car, or your furniture, or your clothing right now? Deduct the loss anyway. In fact, you MUST claim the loss in the year in which it occurred; you cannot delay, except when it's a question of your just discovering the loss (the theft of silverware a year ago, for example), or your trying to salvage something (trees you nursed, but that finally died a few years after a freeze).

Chapter Six
CHARITABLE CONTRIBUTIONS

The big change here is that you no longer can deduct charitable contributions unless you itemize all your deductions on Schedule A, instead of taking the standard deduction. Otherwise, things are pretty much as they were.

In brief, the rules on charitable deductions are:

YOU CANNOT DEDUCT MORE THAN 50 PERCENT OF YOUR ADJUSTED GROSS INCOME IN ONE YEAR. That's a lot of money; few people give that much.

YOU CANNOT DEDUCT MORE THAN 20 PERCENT OF YOUR ADJUSTED GROSS INCOME IN ONE YEAR IF YOU GAVE TO AN ORGANIZATION THAT DOESN'T NORMALLY RECEIVE MUCH SUPPORT FROM THE PUBLIC OR FROM THE GOVERNMENT. Example: a private foundation. This 20 percent limit also applies to gifts of long-term capital-gains property to veterans' organizations, fraternal societies, and nonprofit cemetery companies. If in doubt, check with the organization. But, again, even 20 percent of your adjusted gross income is a big slice, so you probably don't have to worry.

YOU CANNOT DEDUCT MORE THAN 30 PERCENT

OF YOUR ADJUSTED GROSS INCOME IN ONE YEAR IF YOU'RE GIVING LONG-TERM CAPITAL-GAINS PROPERTY. Here, we're talking about giving to charities that ordinarily qualify for the 50 percent limit. Example: You bought 100 shares of IBM at 100; you're donating it at 160. You can deduct $16,000—so long as $16,000 isn't more than 30 percent of your adjusted gross income. And that would be unlikely for most people.

If you gave more than $500, not in cash but in property (like stocks or works of art), you must fill out Form 8283.

If you gave $3,000 or more to any one organization, you must list the gift separately, and identify the organization.

If you made a contribution of over $5,000 and it wasn't either (a) cash or (b) stocks or other publicly traded securities, you must get a signed acknowledgment from the charity. (It's easy to establish the price of stocks traded among the public.) If you've made similar gifts during the year—shares of one particular stock, for example—they will be lumped together, and you may thus exceed the $5,000 limit.

With any gift over $5,000 (other than money or publicly traded securities), you'll also need a written professional appraisal, made within sixty days of your making the gift. (Otherwise, its value may have suddenly plummeted.) Try to get an appraisal early; appraisers become very busy at tax time. And without a note from an appraiser, your gift simply isn't tax-deductible.

You'll also need an appraisal if you donate over $10,000 worth of stock from a closely held corporation—one owned mostly by a small group of people, the shares of which aren't traded to the public. Provide the appraiser's evaluation on Form 8283, and attach it to your return.

The cost of an appraisal isn't deductible as a charitable expense but as a miscellaneous deduction.

As for saving taxes on charitable contributions, we'll begin with a familiar piece of advice:

175 BUNCH YOUR CONTRIBUTIONS.

You can now deduct charitable gifts only if you itemize. So, if you've a mind to, try to contribute more than usual in years when you think you'll be able to itemize, less in the preceding or following years. At the same time, of course, this strategy may ENABLE you to itemize in alternate years.

Let's say that you normally give $2,000 a year to churches or synagogues, United Way, and so forth. If you're sure you'll be able to itemize this year, but possibly not next year, consider giving your usual $2,000 this year—and, at the close of the year, giving the $2,000 you would have contributed next year.

176 REMEMBER YOUR CASH CONTRIBUTIONS.

The cash or checks you contribute—to a church or synagogue, to someone who rings your doorbell collecting for the Girl Scouts or an environmental group—are deductible. Let's hope, though, that you remember these gifts. Ideally, you will have kept records—not just to remind you, but to prove your contribution. Canceled checks or receipts are perfect. The IRS notes that, in the case of small donations of cash, you might produce "items such as buttons, tokens, or emblems that are given to contributors."

Even if you don't have canceled checks or receipts, you may still win the day. One man couldn't prove all his donations to a church, but a court was willing to take his word. The poor man had just been through his second divorce, the court noted, and as so often happens during times of stress, he "looked for solace in the church."

The fact that a person has made generous, documented contributions to charities will help support his or her claims for undocumented contributions.

177 DON'T GIVE PROPERTY WITH LOSSES.

If you bought a stock at 100, and it's now 50, don't give it directly to a charity. Sell it first, then give the proceeds to the charity. That way, you can deduct the loss—either from your capital gains, or from your ordinary income (up to $3,000 a year).

178 GIVE PROPERTY WITH LONG-TERM GAINS.

If you contribute property—typically, stocks—that you owned for six months or less on the day you made the contribution, the profit is considered short-term, and your deduction is limited to what you paid for the property originally. Instead, consider donating property that has long-term gains—you've held it for over six months. The benefit: You won't be taxed on the appreciation. Giving $5,000 worth of property that includes appreciation on which you haven't paid taxes is better than giving $5,000 from your already-taxed income. But he warned that the appreciation may draw the alternate minimum tax upon you. (See Chapter 15.)

179 CARRY OVER ANY EXCESS CONTRIBUTIONS.

If you exceeded the limits on your contributions because they went above the specified percentage of your adjusted gross income, you can carry over the excess to the following year. For example, if your 1987 contributions were $10,000 and this was $1,000 more than half your adjusted gross income, your 1987 deduction is limited to $9,000. The unused $1,000 can be added to your 1988 contributions, subject to the same percentage tests. You have five years to use up such excess charitable contributions.

180 DON'T ATTACH TIGHT STRINGS.

If you attach strings to your gift, you may not be allowed to deduct its value. Let's say you give a computer to a local high school, but stipulate that you must be able to use it three months of the year. No deduction. But if the strings are loose, it's a different story. A man gave his town 800 acres of land, but wanted to keep training his dogs there. Deduction permitted. A deduction was also allowed with regard to a gift of manuscripts to the New York Public Library—despite the proviso that the manuscripts couldn't be copied without the permission of the gift givers.

181 GIVE BEFORE THE END OF THE YEAR.

You cannot deduct a pledge you make this year, promising to fork over the money or assets next year. You'll have to wait until next year for your deduction.

182 WAIT UNTIL THE LAST MINUTE.

If you mail a contribution on December 31, you're considered to have made your gift that year—so long as you used a properly stamped and addressed envelope.

183 DON'T ASSUME ANY GIFT ISN'T DEDUCTIBLE.

You can deduct

• gifts to or for the use of a state, a territory, the United States, or a political subdivision;
• gifts to a domestic fraternal or sororal society if used exclusively for religious or charitable purposes;

• gifts to groups that try to prevent cruelty to children or animals, or that campaign for tolerance of homosexuals or spread information about women's rights;

• gifts to promote national sports competitions if the group doesn't use any of the money to provide athletic facilities or equipment (but your contributions ARE deductible if given to certain amateur sports organizations that do provide athletic facilities or equipment).

The gamut ranges from volunteer fire departments to a state collecting for a parade to accompany a presidential inauguration.

You can even deduct a contribution to reduce the public debt and balance the budget. Submit a check made out to "Bureau of the Public Debt" when you send the IRS your tax return.

In one case, a contribution to a committee to commission a portrait of a new judge for display in a courthouse was held to be deductible.

So is a gift to a nonprofit cemetery corporation to support perpetual care of the lots—so long as it's not for perpetual care of a particular lot (like yours).

When in doubt about whether your contribution is deductible, ask the organization. Don't assume anything. Even a group that tries to influence legislation may be considered a bona fide charity.

184 DON'T GIVE A VALUABLE PAINTING TO A TV STATION.

Give it to an art museum. For you to deduct the full value of your gift, it must go to a group that will use the gift in the course of its ordinary tax-exempt business. Otherwise, your deduction is limited to your gift's original cost.

Even if you present a painting to an art museum, you may be able to deduct only its original cost—if the museum sells your painting within two years. So, when you make such a gift, check what the group plans to do with your present.

185 TAKE A DEDUCTION EVEN IF YOU BENEFIT A BIT.

A man was allowed to deduct a gift to a church—even though the church employed his wife. A doctor was permitted to deduct a lavish gift to a hospital, although his generosity clearly helped spruce up his reputation in the community. And a couple was allowed to deduct contributions to a church even though their son was the church's founder, minister, and president.

Said one judge, "Community goodwill, the desire to avoid community bad will, public pressures of other kinds, tax avoidance, prestige, conscience salving, a vindictive desire to prevent relatives from inheriting family wealth— these are a few of the motives which may lie close to the heart, or so-called heart, of one who gives to charity." But motives don't matter, said the court.

If your motives are just a bit too obvious, though, you may be wiser to take your deduction as a business expense. Example: A cement maker gave to a YMCA's building fund—and he admitted he wanted the YMCA to use HIS cement. He took a business deduction.

186 DON'T THINK THAT ONLY CASH OR CHECKS ARE DEDUCTIBLE.

You can also deduct the cost of clothing, household articles, supplies, and so forth. (To establish their fair market value, try to find what similar items have been selling for recently. If your gift is more than $500, remember, you must fill out Form 8232, and you may need an appraisal.)

One man bought a series of dancing lessons. He contributed them to a charity—and deducted what he had paid. Many land owners have been permitted charitable deductions for stipulating that nothing could be built on their land that would block off the scenic view of the area (a stipulation that lowered the value of their land).

Your own labor, though, is never deductible.

187 DEDUCT THE COST OF TRANSPORTATION.

If you use your car to help out a charitable, religious, or educational group—let's say you drive your Boy Scout group to a baseball game—you can deduct the cost of gas, repairs, tolls, and parking fees. But you can't deduct the car's depreciation or for auto insurance. If you don't want to figure out what percentage of your car's yearly use went to charity, just multiply the mileage you drove the car for charity by 12 cents. You can then ADD parking fees and tolls.

Tax reform cracked down on away-from-home trips, purportedly to help a charity, that were really pleasure trips. (Now no deduction is permissible if the trip included a significant element of personal pleasure, recreation, or vacation.) And tax reform also cracked down on situations where a taxpayer gives a lot of money to a charity, and the charity pays that person to take a "fact-finding trip" to a resort area.

188 DEDUCT THE COST OF INCIDENTALS.

A volunteer nurse can deduct the cost and upkeep of his/her uniform if he/she paid for it him /herself and it's not something he/she could wear elsewhere. The same is true for a Scoutmaster.

189 CHECK INTO THE DEDUCTIBILITY OF CONTRIBUTIONS TO INDIVIDUALS.

Usually, gifts to individuals aren't deductible—the $5 you give to someone who's homeless, for example. But a good

Samaritan who provided lodging, food, and clothing to the victims of a hurricane, under the umbrella of various charitable organizations, was allowed to deduct his costs. Also deductible are reasonable costs for meals and recreation for a child's temporary care if the child was referred by a tax-exempt charitable organization. And a check to a certain missionary was deductible—because the money was for general missionary work.

You can deduct up to $50 per school month for a student—not a dependent or relative—who lives with you. You must have a written agreement with a qualifying organization, like a foreign-exchange group, and you cannot be reimbursed—unless it's just for an unusual event, like the student's stay in a hospital. The student cannot be in college—just in the twelfth grade or lower. Money you spend for the student's books, food, clothing, tuition, and entertainment qualify.

190 GIVE A GROUP GIFT.

If you collect, say, books by one author, see if other collectors will join you in a gift of that author's books to a library. The value of your gifts, together, will probably be more than the value of the gifts individually. That way, all of you can take a greater deduction.

Another example: Three different people gave three parcels of property to a nearby church. The value of the gifts together, divided by three, was worth more than each parcel separately.

191 DEDUCT DUES . . .

along with membership fees, initiation fees, the cost of pew seats, or assessments if they went to a religious group—not to a veterans' organization, country club, or other social group.

192 DEDUCT THE DIFFERENCE BETWEEN THE COST OF A BENEFIT OVER THE REGULAR PRICE.

Ask the sponsors of the event what regular tickets would have cost. If two theater (or sports or film) tickets cost $50 ordinarily, and you paid $100, you can deduct $50. By the same token, you can deduct the difference between the price you pay for an annuity from a tax-exempt group and the annuity's fair market value.

If you buy a ticket to a benefit, and decline to accept the ticket—or donate it back to the charity, or to another charity—you can deduct the full cost.

Chapter Seven
SECURITIES

Tax reform has begun eliminating the favored tax treatment of capital gains—the profits you reap by selling assets such as a stock, a house, a stamp collection, gold, a Siamese cat, or whatever. This is a drastic change. Ever since 1921, the tax code had treated capital gains ever so gently.

In 1987, long-term capital gains (profit on assets you've owned more than six months) are being taxed at a maximum of 28 percent. In 1988 and thereafter, long-term gains will be taxed just the way your salary is—which could be as high as 33 percent. In the good old days (before 1987), the highest rate that long-term gains were taxed at was 20 percent.

But because tax rates are also coming down, many taxpayers will manage to break even. Certainly judging from the behavior of the stock market in the first half of 1987, the harsher treatment of capital gains hasn't discouraged investors. In any case, the people who wrote the tax reform act expressly mentioned the possibility that someday capital gains will once again be treated like a favored child.

To refresh your memory:

If you sold any "capital assets" (gold, stocks, bonds, land) during the year, you must fill out Schedule D. After balancing losses and gains, you put the net gain or loss from your sale or exchange of capital assets on Form 1040.

Losses you have because of selling PERSONAL items aren't deductible at all. Examples: cars, boats, and houses that you don't use in your business. But you can use losses on CAPITAL ASSETS to offset your gains, or even your ordinary income if you don't have other capital gains.

Profits you've made on selling personal items ARE taxable. (I know, it doesn't seem fair.)

Long-term gains are those on assets you've owned over six months. Short-term gains are those on assets you've owned for six months or less. Long-term gains have generally been treated more favorably, and so have short-term losses.

To calculate your net gains or losses, on Schedule D you balance long-term gains against long-term losses; balance short-term gains against short-term losses. Then you offset net long-term gains or losses against net short-term gains or losses.

An important change that tax reform made: You can now use 100 percent of your long-term losses to offset long-term gains, or up to $3,000 a year of ordinary income.

The rule used to be that only 50 percent of long-term losses could be applied against long-term gains, while short-term losses could offset gains, or up to $3,000 a year of ordinary income, dollar for dollar.

If your losses exceed $3,000 a year, carry over what's left to future years. You must use up short-term carryover losses before long-term losses, and earlier losses before later losses.

193 TAKE NET LONG-TERM GAINS IN 1987 . . .

if you expect to be in the 33 percent bracket in 1988, and you have no good investment reason to take your gains in either year. For 1987, the highest tax rate that long-term gains (over six months) are subject to is only 28 percent. If you have a $10,000 long-term gain, the difference between a tax rate of 28 percent ($2,800) and 33 percent is $500.

194 TAKE LONG-TERM GAINS IN 1988 . . .

if you expect to be in the $28,001–$29,750 bracket (married, filing jointly) or the $16,801–$17,850 bracket (filing singly in both 1988 and 1987). Your tax rate on long-term capital gains will fall from 28 percent to 15 percent. That's a big drop. On a $10,000 gain, it represents a difference of $1,300 in taxes.

LONG-TERM CAPITAL GAINS
Married—Joint Return

Taxable Income	Tax Rates	
	1987	1988
$0–$3,000	11%	15%
$3,001–$28,000	15%	15%
$28,001–$29,750	28%	15%
$29,751–$45,000	28%	28%
$45,001–$71,900	28%	28%
$71,901–$90,000	28%	33%
Above $90,000	28%	33%*

Single Return

Taxable Income	Tax Rate	
	1987	1988
$0–$1,800	11%	15%
$1,801–$16,800	15%	15%
$16,801–$17,850	28%	15%
$17,851–$27,000	28%	28%
$27,001–$43,150	28%	28%
$43,151–$54,000	28%	33%
Above $54,000	28%	33%*

*The rate returns to 28% if taxable income exceeds a minimum of $171,090 on a joint return, and $100,480 for a single individual—the exact figure depending on exemptions claimed.

195 CONSIDER TAKING SHORT-TERM GAINS IN 1988.

In 1987, your short-term gains could be taxed as high as 38.5 percent. But next year, tax rates generally are going down; your short-term gains could be taxed at no more than 33 percent, and perhaps 28 percent or 15 percent. So if your gains would remain short-term into next year, and there's no serious danger that your gains would slip away if you waited, hold off. The difference in taxes you would pay if you have a $10,000 gain and you're in the 38.5 percent bracket as against the 28 percent bracket: $1,050.

196 CONSIDER TURNING SHORT-TERM 1987 GAINS INTO LONG-TERM GAINS.

As an alternative, you could hold on to your short-term gains—until they turn into long-term gains.

Let's say that you have a $10,000 short-term gain in 1987, and you're in the 38.5 percent bracket. If you sell, after taxes you would net $6,150. But if you wait until the gain becomes long-term in 1987, you'll pay no more than 28 percent in taxes. Your net profit after taxes would be $7,200—$1,050 more. If you wait until 1988, you'll have the same result. What if you're in the 33 percent bracket in 1988? You'll wind up with $6,700—or $650 more than if you had sold for a short-term gain in 1987.

197 TAKE SHORT-TERM LOSSES IN 1987.

Recall that you use short-term losses to offset short-term gains, then long-term gains, then ordinary income (up to $3,000 a year). Because short-term GAINS will be taxed as high as 38.5 percent in 1987, and short-term losses offset them dollar for dollar, you may be better off taking your short-term losses in 1987. Also consider taking short-term losses in 1987 if you have no long-term gains, in which case your short-term losses will be applied against up to $3,000 of ordinary income.

Of course, if you expect to be in a HIGHER tax bracket in 1988 than in 1987, postpone taking your losses till next year.

As for 1988 and beyond, if you expect to be in the 28 percent bracket in 1988, but the 33 percent bracket in 1989, take your losses in 1989. Whether the gains are short-term or long-term won't matter anymore.

198 TAKE LONG-TERM LOSSES IN 1987.

Before tax reform, only 50 percent of your long-term losses could offset gains or ordinary income. Now 100 percent can. And for the same reason that it's probably better to take short-term losses in 1987, take long-term losses in 1987.

199 SELL FOR A LOSS, AND BUY SOMETHING SIMILAR.

Let's say that you have a loss, and for tax reasons you want to nail down the deduction in the current year. You can sell the stock, and buy it back thirty-one days later—or buy more shares thirty days before you sell the security. (If you or a blood relative bought it back any sooner, you couldn't deduct the loss. It would be a "wash sale.") Even better, sell the security and buy a similar but not "substantially identical" security. That way, you don't have to wait thirty-one days—during which time your ex-stock may soar. If you sell Potomac Electric and buy Hawaii Electric, there's no wash sale; but if you sell a stock and buy the same company's bond that can be converted into the stock, your loss is washed out, and you cannot deduct it. You never need worry about the wash-sale rule if you sell a mutual fund for a loss and buy a similar fund. You could sell Nicholas and buy Nicholas II without being stung by the wash-sale rule because the two funds hold different stocks.

If you buy an option on a stock you've sold, to purchase it back cheaply if it goes up, you're subject to the wash-sale rule if you bought the option within sixty-one days of selling the stock (thirty days before and thirty days after).

What if you give your child money to buy a security you've sold, the child signs a note, and pledges the security as collateral? One court held that you can deduct the loss, even though the child acquired the security within sixty-one days of your selling it.

200 CONSIDER BUYING ON MARGIN.

That means buying securities by borrowing money from your broker. You can deduct all of the interest up to the income you receive from your securities, plus 65 percent more (in 1987) or 40 percent more (in 1988). Limit: $10,000, for a couple filing jointly. In general, you can borrow 50 percent on stocks you buy, 70 percent on bonds, and up to 90 percent on Treasury obligations.

The interest rate you'll pay your broker will be competitive—recently as low as 9 percent or 10 percent. You'll pay a higher rate on debts up to around $50,000.

The danger is that your purchases will go down, and you'll be subject to a "margin call"—a demand that you fork over more cash. If you don't have the cash, your securities will be sold, giving you an automatic loss. Buying on margin, obviously, is only for sophisticated investors.

Incidentally, you're not forced to use your borrowed money to buy securities. If you use the money for personal reasons, you can deduct 65 percent of the interest payments in 1987 and 40 percent in 1988. At 10 percent interest, such a loan would be cheap. But your brokerage firm can call the loan at any time—just to beef up its cash holdings, for example.

201 CUT YOUR LOSSES AND LET YOUR WINNERS RIDE.

This is an investing truism, and it makes sense for tax reasons, too.

The quicker you take losses, the higher your deductions— and the more money you'll have left to invest, save, or spend. And now that you can deduct 100 percent of your long-term losses against gains, and against $3,000 of ordinary income every year, you have more incentive to weed out your losers.

The slower you take gains, the lower your overall tax bill—and, again, the more money you'll have left to do with as you please.

As an investment strategy it makes sense, too. If a stock of yours nose-dives, there's a chance that other investors know something you don't—for example, that the company's sales are turning sour. But if a stock of yours declines along with the market, and your reasons for buying it still apply, you might be wiser to hold on. On balance, it's probably better to sell stocks or other securities if they've fallen 10 percent or 15 percent below your purchase price— simply because of the psychological temptation to hold on, and thus not admit to yourself that you made a mistake buying it in the first place.

If a stock of yours has climbed, it's probably a good idea to hold on. Stocks have momentum. If a company's earnings have risen and business is booming, you can expect the company to continue doing well for a while. But if the stock is a small-company stock, as opposed to a blue chip (from an older, bigger company), it's probably quite volatile. And big ruthless companies may move in to swipe the small company's booming business. You might be more inclined to sell such stocks to lock in your gains.

But don't try to sell out at the exact point when a stock reaches its all-time high. Hardly anyone can do that successfully, time after time. Even the legendary investor Bernard Baruch said, "I always sold too soon." Try for singles; if you always swing for home runs, you'll strike out a lot. And striking out in the investment world is far worse than striking out in baseball.

Granted, many investors do hold stocks too long. They buy a stock at 20, watch it go to 30, and then can't sell—because they greedily hope it will go to 40. They watch in growing dismay as the stock drops back to 20, or even lower, and their profits slip away. As the stock sinks, they become depressed—and, like depressed people in general, they can't act—they can't call their broker and say, "Sell!"

But probably it's even more common for investors to sell too soon. They make a small profit, then hurry to the exit. They continually violate the rule "Sell your losers and let your winners ride"; they hold on to their losers and cut back on their winners. Yet a bank trust officer I know tells me that "Families that have made fortunes have bought good stocks, and held on year after year."

If you simply can't decide whether to sell or hold on, the best solution may be: Sell half your holdings.

As an overall strategy, holding on to your winners makes even more sense, thanks to tax reform.

Beginning in 1988, people have been saying, capital gains will be taxed just like ordinary income—your salary, for instance. But that's not true. An advantage that capital gains still have over ordinary income is that you needn't pay any taxes on them until you actually cash in your assets. And if you hold your gains until you die, your heirs will inherit your holdings—and THEIR cost basis for the assets will generally be the price of the assets on the day you died (or, if they choose, six months after your death). So all of your capital gains—accumulated year after year—can escape taxes. That is one heck of an advantage that capital gains have over ordinary income!

But like all investing rules, there are exceptions. Do sell an asset on which you have a profit if you think that its long-term prospects are dim. Putting a stock in a drawer and never looking at it again isn't appropriate anymore, if it ever once was. Those investors who believe in holding on forever may wind up owning shares of companies that went bankrupt years ago.

202 DON'T FORGET THE CAPITAL-LOSS CARRYOVER.

Check your last year's tax return, Schedule D, to see whether you had capital losses you couldn't entirely use up. These unused losses can be deducted from your current year's capital gains, or from up to $3,000 of ordinary income. (Losses retain their status as long-term or short-term. If you have long-term carryover losses from before 1987, they can offset ordinary income only 50 cents on the dollar.) You can continue to use carryover losses until they're used up, or until you die.

203 ADD BROKERS' COMMISSIONS TO YOUR COST.

When you calculate your gains, add the broker's commission to your basis (total investment). That will lower your taxable gains. If you reinvested dividends to buy more stock, add the small fees that your company charged you. (And remember to use the purchase prices of those shares in calculating your total profits or losses.) The broker's commissions when you sell are deducted from your sale price, and will also reduce your taxable gains.

204 NEVER TREAT INHERITED STOCKS YOU SOLD AS SHORT-TERM GAINS.

Even if you inherited stocks from someone who hadn't held them for over six months, or if you yourself sold the stocks within six months of receiving them, you can treat them as long-term gains. In 1987, this means that the highest tax rate you'll pay on your gains is 28 percent, whereas a short-term gain could be taxed as high as 38.5 percent.

205 DECIDE WHETHER YOU WANT HIGH OR LOW TAXABLE GAINS.

You can—if you bought shares at different times. You can then sell older certificates or newer ones. Usually the older certificates will have the higher gains. But you could have purchased the newer ones when they were real bargains, and thus their gains could be higher.

In a typical situation, an investor needs money, and wants to sell some of his or her holdings. The investor should sell the most recent shares, and thus incur the lower taxes.

But you may want higher gains this year because your tax rate will climb next year, or you have lots of losses to offset against your gains.

Or you may want lower gains now because your tax rate will fall next year (your income is sinking), or you need money and have no losses to offset against them.

If you simply sell your shares, without instructing your broker which to sell (if the broker holds them), or by sending in certificates at random, the IRS will decide that you sold the certificates you bought first. (First in, first out.) With a mutual fund, you don't usually receive certificates. To adjust your gains or losses, instruct the fund or its transfer agent to sell shares you bought on a particular date.

206 SELL LOSING STOCK FUNDS, KEEP WINNERS.

With stock mutual funds, it's probably an even wiser approach to cut your losses and let your winners ride. Afraid that a mutual fund that's done well now owns overpriced stocks, poised for a fall? The portfolio manager may have been smart enough to have sold his or her winners and bought other, undervalued stocks—although the fund's quarterly report doesn't show the switches yet. Hopeful that a fund that's plummeted has underpriced stocks, ready for a rise? The manager may have panicked, sold those low-priced stocks, and purchased recent winners—which are now overpriced.

207 DON'T BUY FUND SHARES RIGHT BEFORE A DISTRIBUTION.

If you send in your investment just before a distribution of capital gains, dividends, or interest, you'll suddenly have taxes to pay on the distribution you've received. This is especially undesirable if you paid in a large amount, and thus received a large taxable distribution. Telephone the fund before you invest, find out when it goes "ex-dividend" (the date when current shareholders are entitled to distributions), and wait a few days before buying shares. The distribution may be made a few days after the ex-dividend date.

208 REMEMBER TO DEDUCT COMMISSIONS.

If you sold mutual funds with either front-end commissions or redemption fees, deduct them from your gains—or add them to your losses. And remember that a fund with a redemption fee may call itself a "no-load" fund.

209 BUY A FUND WITH A LOW TURNOVER.

Such a fund doesn't buy and sell much, so you won't have a lot of capital-gains taxes to pay (assuming the fund's stocks rise). So if two funds you're considering are similar, pay attention to portfolio turnover. One fund with an extraordinarily low turnover: Vanguard Index Trust, because all it does is mirror the S&P 500.

210 REMEMBER THE ADVANTAGES OF TREASURIES.

First, their interest is not taxed by state and local governments. And second, you can defer the taxation of the interest you earn—if you buy an obligation that matures next year, not this.

Of course, Treasuries also happen to be the safest investment in the world, and the interest they pay isn't bad, either. You can usually buy a high-grade corporate bond that pays more, but the interest will be subject to state and local taxes. Municipal bonds usually pay less, though recently they were paying far more than they usually do vis-à-vis Treasuries. And munis, remember, are exempt from FEDERAL taxes, too.

Treasury BILLS are short-term, Treasury NOTES are intermediate-term, and Treasury BONDS are long-term.

The least expensive T-bill is $10,000; beyond that, bills are issued in multiples of $5,000. They mature (come due) in three, six, or twelve months. The longer the maturity, the higher interest they pay—and the greater the risk that you'll be locked in if interest rates in general rise. But while the Treasury Department won't cash in your obligations before maturity, you can sell them early through a bank or broker—at a discount (which can be horribly high).

All Treasury bills (with up to a one-year maturity) are sold at a discount, too. The difference between what you buy them for, and their face value, is your interest—as is true of Series EE savings bonds. For example, if the interest rate on a one-year bill is 10 percent, you can buy a bond with a $10,000 face value, immediately get $1,000 returned to you, and then receive $10,000 a year later.

You can buy Treasury obligations through banks or brokers, for a fee ($25 is typical). You can also buy them directly from a branch of the Federal Reserve near you. For an application, write to the Bureau of the Public Debt, Department of the Treasury, Washington, DC 20239.

Treasury notes usually have maturities from two to ten years. Those maturing in less than four years have minimum denominations of $5,000; those maturing in four years or more, $1,000. Interest is paid twice a year.

Treasury bonds have maturities extending from over ten years to thirty years. Minimum denomination: $1,000. Interest is paid twice a year.

211 DON'T OVERLOOK SERIES EE SAVINGS BONDS.

Remember when savings bonds were low-paying, dull investments? No more.

Today, Series EE savings bonds are hot items. One reason: They're exempt from state and local taxes, which have been climbing. Another: Their earnings can be tax-deferred—for at least twelve years, when they mature. Finally, if inflation returns, the interest on Series EE bonds may keep apace because the rates are changed every six months, in line with the rates on five-year Treasury securities.

Savings bonds have become an especially good purchase for children, now that family income-shifting possibilities have been cut back. You can buy bonds for a 2-year-old child; they will mature in twelve years, when the child is fourteen. At that time, their accumulated interest will be taxed at the child's low rates, not yours. Of course, if the child has little other investment income, there's no reason for the child to defer paying taxes on the bonds. Up to $500 of a child's unearned income is untaxed, and up to $500 is taxed at the child's rate, not at the parents' rate.

Series EE bonds are also suitable for someone nearing retirement: The would-be retiree can invest in the bonds, and get the entire accumulated interest when he or she retires and very likely is in a lower tax bracket.

Currently if you hold a bond for five years or longer, the interest rate is 6 percent, which isn't bad, especially if you live in a state with high taxes. And the rate will rise as the rate on five-year Treasuries rises. Every 6 months, the Treasury sets the savings bond rate at 85 percent of the market yield on five-year Treasury securities for the previous half year.

EE bonds sell at a discount from their face value. A $50 bond, for instance, sells for $25. At maturity, you receive the $50.

You cannot buy Series EE bonds with a face value of more than $30,000 in any calendar year in any one person's name. You cannot use them as collateral for a loan. You cannot cash them in during the first six months.

To purchase savings bonds, visit banks, savings and loan associations, or Federal Reserve Banks, or buy them through your employer's payroll savings plan.

Don't confuse Series EE bonds with Series HH bonds, whose interest rate is fixed. HH bonds provide current interest. You can buy Series HH bonds only with at least $500 of Series EE or the older E bonds. You cannot buy them directly. Unlike EE bonds, with HH bonds there's no reduction in the interest rate if you cash them in early.

The bonds mature in ten years, but the interest is reportable each year.

212 SELL NEWER EE BONDS FIRST.

If you need cash and have old as well as new savings bonds to sell, sell the newer ones. Because your newer bonds have less accumulated interest, cashing them in won't add as much to your tax bill.

213   DEFER PAYING TAXES ON SERIES EE BONDS PAST THEIR MATURITY.

You can, by using them to buy HH bonds, and thus postponing paying taxes on your accumulated Series EE earnings. You can hold the HH bonds until they mature in ten years, or until you decide to cash them in. With the older E bonds, you could just hold them past their maturity, and still postpone taxes on their accumulated interest. The Treasury hasn't decided on whether you can do this with Series EE bonds.

214   BUY VARIOUS DENOMINATIONS OF SAVINGS BONDS.

If you cash in a bond before five years, the interest rate becomes very low. That's why you shouldn't buy a few bonds with high face values. Instead, buy a variety of smaller bonds, so that if you need immediate cash, you won't have to cash in your big bonds and wind up with a low interest rate on a lot of money.

215   DON'T FORGET TO DEDUCT CORPORATE/MUNICIPAL BOND LOSSES . . .

if you sold them for less than you bought them. The same goes for bonds you bought at a premium (above their original selling price): When they mature, you can deduct a loss. By the same token, you must pay capital-gains taxes on your bonds if you sold them before they matured, for MORE than you paid.

216   YOU CAN AVOID THE WASH-SALE RULE IF . . .

you sell a bond and, within thirty-one days, buy a bond issued by the same company but with a very different interest rate. Just buying a bond issued by the same company but with a different MATURITY date is risky. You may not be able to deduct your loss.

217 CONSIDER SINGLE-STATE MUNI FUNDS.

If you live in a state with high state taxes (like New York, California, Ohio, Minnesota, and Maryland), consider a mutual fund that buys only municipals issued in your state. Your interest will probably escape state and local taxes as well as federal taxes. For the names of such funds, contact the Investment Company Institute in Washington, DC.

218 CONSIDER BONDS ISSUED BY THE TERRITORIES.

Such bonds, along with those issued by Puerto Rico and the District of Columbia, are exempt from taxes in all states. Talk with a stockbroker.

219 DECIDE WHAT INTEREST RATE WOULD APPEAL TO YOU.

To determine whether a tax-exempt or a taxable bond makes economic sense for you, check what taxable bonds (like corporates) are paying now, then estimate your top tax rate. If your top rate—your "marginal" rate—will be 28 percent in 1988, for example, a taxable bond would have to yield 11.11 percent to equal a muni yielding 8 percent.

Taxable Versus Tax-Exempt Bonds

To equal a municipal bond yielding:	5%	6%	7%	8%	9%
If you're in the 15% marginal tax bracket, a taxable bond must yield	5.88%	7.06%	8.24%	9.41%	10.59%
If you're in the 28% marginal tax bracket, a taxable bond must yield	6.94%	8.33%	9.72%	11.11%	12.5%
If you're in the 33% marginal tax bracket, a taxable bond must yield	7.46%	8.95%	10.44%	11.94%	13.4%

220 CONSIDER ZERO COUPON BONDS.

They can be ideal for pension plans like IRAs and for saving for a child's college education.

Zeros may be based on corporate bonds, Treasury obligations, or municipal bonds. They're fixed-income investments that don't pay you interest until the principal becomes due.

You can buy zeros at a small fraction of their eventual redemption value, which will include their principal as well as all of their accumulated interest.

Although you won't receive interest on your zero bond, every year you'll have to pay taxes on the interest you've deferred.

You can purchase a $1,000 zero for as little as $100 or $200—the price depends on when it comes due and the yield. Because you must pay fees—2 percent to 5 percent of the purchase price—shop around among brokers and bankers for the best deal.

One benefit of zeros is that you know exactly how much you'll receive when they mature—whether in ten years or thirty years. Also, you don't have to decide how to reinvest the interest: You don't receive any until the zero comes due. Finally, a zero is a way to force yourself to save money.

Taxable zeros—from the corporate bonds or Treasuries—are suitable for pension plans like IRAs and Keoghs, because you won't have to pay the "imputed" interest over the years (the interest you don't receive).

Tax-exempt zeros—based on municipal bonds—are suitable for saving for a child's college education. Even when they mature, you or your child won't owe any taxes.

One drawback of zeros is that, because they're long-term, their principal can fluctuate wildly over the years, depending on current interest rates. If you must cash them in early, and interest rates have climbed, you may be shocked at how much their value has sunk. Of course, if interest rates have gone down, you can cash in a zero early—at a profit.

Chapter Eight
INSURANCE

Making an investment through an insurance policy may seem peculiar, but it's been done for years—by means of whole-life insurance. And now tax reform has helped make whole-life insurance, along with annuities, among the most intriguing investments around.

Reason: These two insurance-company products (which we'll explain below) have emerged from tax reform almost unscratched. The money you put into whole-life insurance or annuities can still appreciate year after year without being taxed.

If you're among those people who can't deduct an IRA contribution anymore, why not use a (nondeductible) insurance investment to shield your retirement money from taxes? And why be limited to a piddling $2,000 a year when you can salt away as much as $5 million a year?

And because you no longer can move much money into your kids' low brackets to save for their college educations, why not sprinkle money into an insurance policy that lets you invest in a tax-shielded mutual fund—and borrow your investment at a low interest rate, or even free of charge?

If you think all this sounds too good to be true, you're right. Annuities and life insurance are glamorous, but they have sharp thorns:

• Comparing policies is dizzyingly difficult. The insurance industry hasn't standardized the provisions, and the possible permutations and combinations seem infinite.

• As a result, getting reliable advice is a problem. Even some of the very best financial planners say they're sticking to selling simple-term insurance—because they don't understand all "the other stuff."

• The policies themselves are strewn with fees and charges, even though they may be described as "no loads." In fact, these fees and charges cut deeply into the benefits of tax deferral.

But at this point, let's pause for a somewhat oversimplified crash course in life insurance and annuities.

Once upon a time, you had mainly a choice between term and whole-life (also called cash-value) insurance. "Term" is pure insurance—plain vanilla, with no artificial flavoring. You don't make any kind of investment; the premiums rise as you grow older. "Whole-life" insurance, which costs far more, comes with a savings account. The premiums remain level.

The trouble with whole-life is that (1) the sales charges are enormous—sometimes as much as half the first year's premium; (2) the savings account pays little—maybe 5 percent; and (3) the insurance company uses the cash value to keep the premium unchanging. So, when you die, your beneficiaries receive only the face amount of the policy. (If you borrow your cash value, your insurance coverage is reduced.) And the fact that the premiums don't rise isn't really helpful. The young need lots of insurance, not high premiums; older people can better afford higher premiums, but—in any case—usually need less life insurance.

"Universal" life insurance is an improved version of cash-value insurance. The savings account grows at a competitive interest rate (now about 8 percent). And you have a lot of flexibility: You can allot your premiums between the cash value and insurance, and even change the size and frequency of your premiums. But even with most universal-life policies, your savings account is lost if you die.

"Variable" life insurance entered the scene in 1976. Here, your savings account varies—the rate of return isn't fixed. The reason is that your money can be invested in a variety of mutual funds, including stock funds, depending upon your choice. (This is somewhat risky, of course, but the stock market is where big money can be made.)

While your heirs don't receive the cash value of a variable policy when you die, you insurance coverage grows in step with the cash value. So your heirs don't lose all of your appreciation if you die while holding on to the policy: The policy's face value reflects the appreciation.

Another innovation is "single premium" variable life insurance. You invest a lump sum—as little as $5,000 or as much as $5 million, but typically $50,000 or so. Depending on your age, your premium buys two to ten times the amount in insurance protection. Usually you can borrow up to 75 percent of the cash value during the first two or three years, and 90 percent thereafter. If you borrow only the appreciation, you may be charged no interest at all; borrow the principal as well, and you may be charged 1 percent to 4 percent a year.

Annuities have also undergone major changes. Once they were just a form of insurance that protected you in case you lived as long as Methuselah. You paid in your money, and later on you received a yearly stipend, as long as you lived—even if the insurance company lost money on the deal.

The key drawback of annuities was that the stipend could be shrunk by inflation. But now you can buy variable annuities, attached to stock mutual funds, which can keep your stipend in line with normal inflation.

Unfortunately, unlike variable life, you cannot borrow from an annuity without owing income taxes.

Clearly, whole-life life insurance and annuities are well

worth considering. But you must make some difficult choices.

221 CONSIDER INSURANCE-BASED INVESTMENTS RATHER THAN A MUNI FUND.

Both a municipal-bond fund and insurance-based investments provide tax-free accumulations.

A muni-bond fund has certain advantages. You can get your money out quickly, and without special penalties. (With the insurance policies, the company may hit you with a surrender charge if you withdraw your investment in the first few years.) And if you withdraw your money from a muni fund, you won't owe taxes on the interest.

But with the insurance products, you may get a higher return. The insurer can invest in high-paying corporate bonds, for example, as well as stocks. Also, if you die, the proceeds of both annuities and life insurance escape the costs of probate courts. With annuities, your heirs owe income taxes only on the appreciation; with life insurance, all proceeds are untaxed. That's not the case with a muni fund or other investments.

Of course, there's nothing wrong with having both a muni fund and insurance investments.

222 CONSIDER A VARIABLE ANNUITY IF YOU'RE YOUNG.

Younger people might opt for a variable annuity, choosing greater risk for possibly greater rewards. At their age, they can wait out any stock-market declines. Older people might lean toward a fixed annuity, because they might need money just when the stock market is in the doldrums. Again, there's no rule against having both types of annuities.

223 CONSIDER SINGLE-PREMIUM WHOLE LIFE IF YOU'RE OLDER.

Single-premium policies don't have the enormous commissions of typical whole-life policies. And they're suitable for older people, who want a conservative investment and a regular income, which they can get by withdrawing their interest—without borrowing charges or taxes.

224 CHOOSE VARIABLE LIFE FOR FLEXIBILITY.

Life insurance has a key advantage over an annuity: You can borrow your savings account without tax consequences. If you withdraw money from an annuity before you're fifty-nine and a half, and you're not disabled or you don't annuitize the payments, you'll have a 10 percent tax penalty on the amount you've withdrawn.

On the other hand, you'll pay extra for the insurance coverage of life policies—and you may not need any more insurance.

Yet variable life may be better even if you pay for insurance you don't need, simply because of your access to the cash value. But if you don't expect you'll need to borrow any money, and you're definitely saving just for retirement, a variable annuity is probably better.

225 CONSIDER VARIABLE INSURANCE ALONG WITH NO-LOAD MUTUAL FUNDS.

Most no-load funds have lower expenses and fees than variable annuities and variable life. But the insurance-based funds do protect your profits from taxes—year after year.

Regular mutual funds are easy to track and to compare—their records are listed in newspapers. That's not the case with insurance-based funds. Still, if your insurance-based stock fund has performed poorly, you can usually transfer to sister money-market or bond funds; you can even switch from one insurance company's policy to another, without tax consequences. Besides, some mutual funds linked with insurance products have done splendidly.

All in all, it's probably best to diversify—to have some of your funds in no-load funds and some in variable insurance policies and variable annuities. (See Appendix C for a comparison of various ways to invest in stock mutual funds.)

226 CHOOSE AN ANNUITY CAREFULLY.

Buy from insurance companies rated A+ by the A.M. Best Company. (Check a library for *Best's Reports*, or ask insurance agents.)

If you're purchasing a fixed and not a variable annuity, find out the initial interest rate, and see how long it's guaranteed. Inquire about early-withdrawal fees: You want them to vanish in a few years, not in ten years. If you're purchasing a variable annuity, look for one managed by an investment company with a good record—such as Fidelity, Merrill Lynch, Value Line, Vanguard, or Twentieth Century.

227 CHOOSE A VARIABLE LIFE POLICY CAREFULLY.

Again, look for policies from companies rated A+ by the A.M. Best Company, and funds managed by investment companies with glittering reputations. (Any fund open to the general public cannot be offered in a variable policy, so you cannot buy—for example—a famous fund like Fidelity Magellan via an insurance policy.)

228 DON'T ABUSE SINGLE-PREMIUM LIFE INSURANCE.

Investors may be tempted to borrow from their policies to the hilt, lowering their insurance coverage and possibly dissipating their savings.

But apart from the danger that people will abuse the policies, single-premium variable life is tempting—especially if you need more life insurance and you can spring for a large sum, like $50,000. When you invest that much, the fees and expenses are relatively low. And if you want to save for a child's education, a neat way to do it is to buy a policy on your life, then borrow against it later on.

229 MAKE UP YOUR MIND FAIRLY QUICKLY.

A case can be made that an investor should wait—until the insurance industry standardizes its products, makes them more understandable, and (owing to competition) lowers the high fees and expenses.

Then again, perhaps you shouldn't wait. Congress may decide to start taxing loans from single-premium life insurance. It may also decide to start taxing the "inside buildup" of all cash-value insurance policies, the way Canada does. But if you invest now, you may be grandfathered in should Congress ever take away the intriguing appeal of insurance-based investments.

Chapter Nine
REAL ESTATE

Tax reform has cut back on the generous benefits of investing in real estate. Yet some advantages remain, and investors can still profit from them handsomely.

To begin with, we'll offer tips on how to cope with the changes. Then we'll relay some time-honored strategies that still work, despite tax reform. (Many of the suggestions were provided by Martin M. Shenkman, a lawyer and CPA who wrote *Real Estate After Tax Reform*, published by John Wiley & Sons.)

230 AVOID PERMANENT IMPROVEMENTS, EMPHASIZE REPAIRS.

Under tax reform, residential real estate put in use after 1986 must be depreciated over the course of 27.5 years, and other real estate over 31.5 years; accelerated depreciation, which is more liberal than straight-line depreciation, is no longer permitted on new property.

You cannot immediately deduct the cost of an improvement; all you can do is depreciate the cost, or add it to your basis (total investment). But you can deduct the cost of repairs in the year you make them. That's why you should emphasize repairs.

True, the line between improvements and repairs can be narrow. (One well-known accounting firm claims that a new roof constitutes a repair; other tax authorities I've interviewed are dubious, and the IRS itself specifically calls a new roof an improvement.) In general, though, if you maintain your property the way you should, you are in the bailiwick of repairs—and you may not be forced to make many nondeductible improvements.

Consider sealing, patching, or repaving a driveway instead of installing a new one. Think about repairing your furnace or water heater instead of splurging on new models. Instead of having a house renovated all at once, have it painted one year, new carpets installed the next, and new wallpaper put up the third year. If you have everything done at once, the IRS may consider it an improvement, not a series of repairs.

231 DEPRECIATE PERSONAL PROPERTY FASTER.

You can still depreciate "personal property" over just five or seven years—faster than you can depreciate "real property." (Personal property: furniture, equipment, and such. Real property: the building and its structural parts.) And with personal property, you can still use accelerated depreciation—deducting more during the early years, less later on.

232 MAKE ANY ADDITIONS PERSONAL PROPERTY.

The key distinction: Personal property is easily movable. So make your additions movable. Instead of nailing down a carpet or tiles, attach it with special removable glue. Put up a ready-made bookcase; don't install a built-in bookcase.

233 LEASE THE LAND.

If you buy the house or factory but rent the land, more of your investment can be depreciated. (Land cannot be depreciated.) And you can immediately deduct your rental payments for the land.

234 IF YOU EXPECT LOSSES, LOWER YOUR ADJUSTED GROSS INCOME.

Under tax reform, losses from rental property are deductible in full only from other "passive" income (like income from limited partnerships), not from "active" income (wages) and portfolio income (dividends and interest). A major exception: You can deduct up to $25,000 in losses from active or portfolio income IF (a) your adjusted gross income is under $100,000, (b) you "actively" manage your property, and (c) you own at least 10 percent of the property. (From $100,000 to $150,000, you lose the deductions, at a rate of $1 for every $2 of income.) If you bought the property before October 26, 1986, you can deduct 65 percent of excess losses from ordinary or portfolio income in 1987, 20 percent in 1988, 10 percent in 1990, and none in 1991 and afterward. Losses beyond these percentages can be carried over to succeeding years. When you sell, you can offset any gains with these carryover losses.

The maximum $25,000 deduction is, oddly enough, the same whether you are married or single. But if a married couple living together file separately, they lose the deduction. If they live apart and file separately, the deduction is cut in half. (The IRS wants to discourage marrieds from filing separate returns.)

So if you expect to have nondeductible losses, try to keep your adjusted gross income as low as you can—by funding your deductible pension plans to the hilt, for example.

(IRAs, in this case, won't lower your adjusted gross income.)

235   LOWER YOUR INCOME IN ALTERNATE YEARS.

The result will be that, in those alternate years, you may be below the $100,000 floor. Postpone, or speed up, receiving income—from bonuses, commissions, sales, whatever. In 1987, you might try to accelerate income normally scheduled for 1988—because, in 1987, 65 percent of excess passive losses remain deductible from other kinds of income.

236   PROVE THAT YOU ACTUALLY MANAGE YOUR PROPERTY.

Even if you use a rental agent, you should approve new tenants, okay improvement or repair expenses over $100 or $200, decide on rental terms, sign original or renewal leases, keep copies of paperwork. In a folder, store your notes about conversations with your agent or tenants, and memos about visits to your property. (If you're buying property in the first place, it should be within an hour's drive, so you can more easily prove you're an active manager.)

237   CONSIDER USING YOUR SUMMER HOME MORE.

If you have paper losses from renting a vacation home and you can no longer fully deduct them from nonpassive income, consider spending more time there yourself. You can deduct a greater portion of the property taxes and mortgage interest (if you itemize).

238   CONSIDER SELLING YOUR PROPERTY IN 1987 OR TRADE YOUR HOLDINGS.

Long-term capital gains are losing their favored status after 1987. So, if you're thinking of selling for a profit either in

1987 or 1988, you might be better off selling earlier. In 1987, the highest tax rate on your long-term gains is 28 percent, but the rate could be 33 percent next year. If you're selling for a loss, consider selling in 1987 if you're in a high tax bracket (35 percent or 38.5 percent).

As an alternative to selling for a profit, trade your holdings for similar property. That way, you can defer paying taxes on the gain.

Such a tax-free trade must involve "like-kind" property—like land in exchange for a shopping center, but not a house for an airplane. Both properties must have been held for business or investment purposes. Your new mortgage must equal or exceed the mortgage on the property you're trading. The property you're to receive must be identified within forty-five days of your transferring your own property. The exchange itself must be completed within 180 days after the transfer of the first property—or the extended due date of your tax return, if earlier.

You can trade a ranch in this country for a ranch abroad; unimproved land (not depreciable) for improved land (partly depreciable).

Warning: If you've fully depreciated your own property, you cannot depreciate the new property.

239 PETITION THE RENT-CONTROL BOARD.

If your dwellings are subject to rent control, ask the rent-control board to reconsider the rents you're allowed to charge, in view of your reduced tax benefits.

240 DON'T DEPRECATE DEPRECIATION.

A landlord I have heard of, a woman who knows little about taxes, doesn't charge the tenants in her home any rent. She just assesses them a portion of the house's expenses—the taxes, mortgage interest, operating expenses. This way, she thinks, she can avoid having to file complicated tax returns. She also figures that she'll make money on the appreciation of her house.

She's making two mistakes. First, the payments that her tenants make are income she's receiving—and she must report such payments. Second, she's missing out on depreciation, which—despite tax reform—can still make her a nifty profit. In fact, being able to depreciate real estate is a cardinal reason why, over the years, so many investors in real estate have grown wealthy.

Depreciation is the regular deduction of the cost of a business asset over its lifetime because it's supposedly losing value as it grows older—like a typewriter you use in your work. If a business asset of yours has a five-year life, for tax purposes, you can deduct 20 percent of its value every year. (A typewriter supposedly has a five-year life.) This is called "straight-line" depreciation. If you could deduct a higher percentage during an asset's early years, and a lesser percentage later on, it would be "accelerated" depreciation. Accelerated is usually better; you save more money, sooner.

Most real estate appreciates; it doesn't actually depreciate—until it gets VERY old. So the depreciation deduction is just a special benefit that real-estate investors enjoy.

In the good old days, you could depreciate residential and commercial real estate over nineteen years. Tax reform, as mentioned, has lengthened the time. But depreciation is still something no landlord should dispense with. Depreciation isn't all it used to be, but what's left should be very much appreciated.

241 BUYERS SHOULD EMPHASIZE INTEREST, NOT PRICE.

Thanks to tax reform, when you buy property now, it may be better to pay less for the property, and pay higher interest. Remember that now you must depreciate property

over a longer period of time, using straight-line depreciation, whereas you can deduct interest payments much
sooner. As for sellers, with the distinction between capital
gains and interest income being wiped out, whether they
receive a higher price or higher interest may not matter so
much.

242 START DEPRECIATING AS EARLY AS YOU CAN AND DELAY PURCHASES OF PERSONAL PROPERTY WHEN YOU'RE NEAR $200,000.

You needn't wait until a tenant actually moves in, or the
day he or she signs the lease. When the building is available
for rental, and you're trying to rent it, generally you can
start depreciating it.

You can write off up to $10,000 per item of personal
property you use in your business in the year you buy it.
This benefit is phased out, dollar for dollar, when your
investments exceed $200,000. (The $10,000 write-off is
sometimes called "expensing" or the Section 179 deduction.)

So that you can continue to deduct up to $10,000 per
item, try to delay purchasing some assets to the early part
of next year if you're nearing the $200,000 limit.

243 RENT TO A RELATIVE.

You'll still qualify for tax benefits, so long as the property
is your relative's main residence, and the rent is set at the
fair market value. You'll have a regular tenant who won't
skip in the middle of the night, venting any anger by
trashing up the place; your relative will have a kind, understanding landlord.

244 DON'T OVERLOOK DEDUCTIBLE EXPENSES.

Besides depreciation, there's fire insurance, liability insurance, advertising for tenants, cleaning services, travel expenses (including meals and lodgings when you visit rental property outside your area), legal, architectural, and accounting fees, supplies, water, fuel, taxes. And there's maintenance—repainting, repapering, fixing leaks, repairing plumbing and wiring, extermination, and so forth.

245 DEDUCT RENTAL EXPENSES EVEN IF YOU DON'T ITEMIZE.

Use Schedule E to deduct your rental expenses from your rental income.

246 CONSIDER BUYING A VACATION HOME.

In some ways, tax reform has made vacation homes especially attractive.

If your adjusted gross income is below $100,000, you actively manage the property, and the place qualifies as a rental residence, you can write off up to $25,000 of any tax losses from the rentals against active income (your salary) and against portfolio income (dividends and interest). But mortgage interest linked to your personal use of the property will be considered consumer interest—only partially deductible over the next few years.

On the other hand, if it's a personal residence, and only your second home (not your third or fourth), you can deduct all your home mortgage payments and property taxes— providing the mortgage isn't for more than the original purchase price plus improvements. (You can borrow against the appreciation and deduct the interest if you obtained the loan before August 16, 1986, or you use the proceeds for educational or medical expenses, home improvements, or your business.) But if yours is a personal and not rental residence, expenses connected with any rental period can be deducted only up to the amount of your rental income. (Any excess losses can be carried forward to a time when you have excess rental income, or you sell the place.)

If your vacation home doesn't qualify as your second home, your interest is considered consumer interest, and you can deduct only 65 percent in 1987, 40 percent in 1988, 20 percent in 1989, 10 percent in 1990, and nothing thereafter.

If you rent out the home for less than fifteen days in the year, you need not report the rental income—though you won't be able to deduct any rental expenses, either. (The IRS just wants to eliminate the red tape involved.) So, if your vacation home is in a resort area, or an area that has a popular event once a year, seriously think of renting it for fourteen days. You can still deduct interest, taxes, and casualty/theft losses for those fourteen days.

How do you determine whether your vacation home is a rental or a personal residence, if you use it as both?

If you yourself use the home for (a) more than two weeks, or (b) more than 10 percent of the rental time, whichever is longer, it's a personal residence. Your deductions for maintenance and depreciation for the rental period are limited to the rental income, minus property taxes and interest for the rental period.

The IRS calculates the maintenance and depreciation expenses for the rental period by taking the same percentages of these expenses as the rental period is to the total time of use by the owner and by the renter. The IRS measures the amount of property taxes and interest, which reduce rental income, the same way.

But tax courts disagree with the IRS on how to calculate the property taxes and interest that reduce the rental income. The courts divvy up the taxes and interest in proportion to the entire year rather than in proportion to the total period of use.

In general, you're better off using the tax-court method when your vacation home qualifies as a personal residence; you're better off using the IRS method when your vacation home qualifies as a rental property.

247 DECIDE WHICH IS BETTER FOR YOU—RENTAL OR PERSONAL PROPERTY.

The answer depends in part on how much you want to use the property for yourself. As mentioned, it's a personal residence if you use it for more than fourteen days of the year—or more than 10 percent of the number of days the vacation home is rented, if that's a higher number. So if you rent the home for three hundred days, you could live there thirty days—and it still wouldn't be considered a personal residence, because you didn't exceed the 10 percent limit. You could deduct rental expenses up to your rental income.

Your answer will also depend, in large part, on whether your adjusted gross income is over $100,000–$150,000. If that's the case, you won't be able to deduct all your tax losses. You may be wiser to use your second home as a personal residence, so as to be able to deduct all the mortgage interest.

If your adjusted gross income is below $100,000, and you actively manage the place, you may prefer to use tax deductions to lower your active and portfolio income. In that case, don't spend more than fourteen days there—or more than 10 percent of the days you rent out the home. The mortgage interest for the time you yourself spend in the home would be fully deductible, up to the purchase price of the home plus improvements.

248 DON'T COUNT MAINTENANCE DAYS AS PERSONAL DAYS.

Any days you spend working on your vacation home aren't considered personal days, and thus don't reduce your fourteen-day limit. They don't count as rental days, either. You can bring along friends and relatives, who lazily decline to pitch in, and STILL not include the day as a personal day.

249 IF YOU'RE A GUEST, IT'S STILL A RENTAL DAY.

Your tenants invite you to spend a day or two at your own rental house. The day or two remain rental days. Lesson: Be friendly with your tenants.

250 REMEMBER TO DEDUCT CASUALTY LOSSES IN FULL.

With rental property, you can deduct all casualty or theft losses. They're not subject to the $100 reduction and the reduction of 10 percent of your adjusted gross income.

251 PERSUADE TENANTS TO MOVE IN SOONER.

If you're just starting to rent property, persuade the tenants to move in as soon as possible—so you can start depreciating the building as soon as possible, with no argument from the IRS about when the property was put into use.

252 BE CAREFUL WHAT YOU WRITE IN YOUR LEASE.

If you require a tenant to restore your property to the exact condition in which he or she received it, you may not be entitled to a depreciation deduction. Write in your lease that the premises must be restored to their original condition, but subject to ordinary wear and tear.

253 DON'T REPORT A SECURITY DEPOSIT AS INCOME . . .

if you accepted the deposit strictly to protect yourself against damage the tenants might cause. It would become income only if you use it and don't return it. And if you used it for repairs, you could deduct the repair expenses, up to the amount of the security deposit you used. To ensure that the deposit isn't considered advance income, be sure that your lease calls for a deposit equal to one (or more) month's rent, not IN LIEU of the final month's rent.

If you're required to pay interest on the security deposit, it's usually not considered advance income.

254 MAKE THE TENANT LIABLE FOR ANY PENALTY.

Let's say that a tenant brings in so many other tenants, without your approval, that he/she infringes the zoning code, and you must pay a penalty. The tenant reimburses you, but you must declare that payment as income. And you can't deduct the penalty.

To get around this, your lease should hold the tenant directly responsible for any penalties.

255 DON'T DECLARE ANY IMPROVEMENTS YOUR TENANT MADE.

If your tenant painted, or wallpapered, or installed a bookcase, and left everything there when he or she left, don't declare the tenant's generosity as income. These are pure gifts—providing that they weren't a substitute for rent the tenant owed.

256 BOOST THE BASIS OF YOUR RAW LAND.

You can add to the land's basis (total investment) any interest and taxes you pay, if you don't itemize. They'll lower your taxable profit when you sell.

257 CONSIDER REITS.

With tax rates dropping, and with capital gains taxed exactly like ordinary income in 1988, you may be more interested in income-producing investments. If that's the case, consider real estate investment trusts. Like mutual funds, they invest in a variety of real-estate ventures—from mortgages to properties. They're traded on stock exchanges, so you have liquidity. And if they pass along most of their profits to shareholders, REITs (pronounced REETS) aren't subject to federal taxes—so there's more money for YOU.

REITs that invest in properties generally have more potential for capital gains; those that invest in mortgages generally pay higher dividends.

REITs may be the cheapest way to invest in real estate. You can just buy shares of those traded on stock exchanges.

258 CONSIDER REMICS.

These are new mortgage-backed securities created by tax reform. The name stands for Real Estate Mortgage Investment Conduit. REMICs will pay competitive interest rates. And the income from a REMIC won't be taxed twice—first, as it's received, then as you the shareholder receive it. Only you, the shareholder, will normally be taxed on the income. That's one reason why the yield should be high. Your income, by the way, will be passive income—the kind that can be offset by tax losses from your other real estate or limited partnerships. You should be hearing a lot more about REMICs soon.

259 CONSIDER LIMITED PARTNERSHIPS.

Limited partnerships were once known as tax shelters; thanks to tax reform, they're just limited partnerships again. Still, if you have "passive" losses, naturally you'll think of getting passive income, probably through limited partnerships. But be sure, this time around, that your investment is economically sound.

Even without their former tax benefits, limited partnerships are suitable for real-estate investors seeking high profits and not eager to have all the annoyances that landlords have. Many partnerships have been restructured to emphasize income, not deductions. And these days, many partnerships are offering a degree of liquidity, with firms arranging to buy out investors' shares. Even so, limited partnerships are mainly for long-term investors. One reason is that fees and commissions are high—20 percent to 30 percent of your original investment, typically.

Most public partnerships charge a minimum of $5,000; most private partnerships—not registered with the Securities and Exchange Commission, and restricted to wealthy investors—have minimums of $25,000.

Unlike regular corporations, limited partnerships can pass along profits and losses directly to shareholders.

260 CONSIDER INVESTING IN LOW-INCOME HOUSING.

If you qualify, you can get tax credits for providing housing for people with low incomes, and these credits can offset active as well as portfolio income, not just passive income. For new construction and for the rehabilitation of buildings put into use in 1987, a credit is available at a rate of 9 percent of your expenses, provided the project isn't financed with tax-exempt bonds and isn't government-subsidized; for acquiring an existing building, the credit is 4 percent. The credits are available for ten years. After 1987, the credit rates will be changed every month to mirror market interest rates. Investors who have already bought into low-income housing may still be able to deduct passive losses from active income and portfolio income.

Investors with adjusted gross income of up to $200,000 can use credits to deduct up to $25,000 of other income a year. You lose a $1 deduction for every $2 that your income goes from $200,000 to $250,000.

261 CONSIDER FIXING UP OLD OR HISTORIC BUILDINGS.

Again, you can get credits to offset other income—active as well as portfolio. If the building is historic—named in the *National Register of Historic Landmarks*, a list of properties designated as historic by the Department of the Interior—and your rehabilitative work meets with the Department of the Interior's approval, your credit is 20 percent of eligible costs. (Property also may qualify if it's in an area certified by your state as a historic district.) After the work is done, you cannot live in the property yourself if you want a tax credit; you must use it as your place of business, or rent it out.

If it's an ordinary old building, put in use before 1936, your credit is 10 percent of your rehabilitative costs. While historic buildings can be residential or commercial for you to qualify for the credit, the ordinary old buildings must be nonresidential. As with historic property, you cannot live in the property and be entitled to the credit.

Chapter Ten
HOMEOWNERS

The tax benefits of owning your own home, condominium, cooperative, houseboat, or whatever have been nicked by tax reform, but not grievously wounded. Homeowners still enjoy delicious deductions that renters don't—for local real-estate taxes, and (with limits) mortgage interest payments. And there are all sorts of other wonderful blessings that Uncle Sam bestows upon homeowners, just to encourage Americans to join the club. So our first piece of advice is . . .

262 BECOME A HOMEOWNER.

If a homeowner decides to borrow money to buy a car, pay a medical expense or tuition bills, or even traipse off to Tahiti, he or she may be able to deduct ALL the interest charged—by means of a home-equity loan. Renters can deduct only a shrinking percentage of such interest.

That's not all. The favored fraternity of homeowners may also (1) postpone paying capital-gains taxes on their profit when they sell their houses, or perhaps never have to pay a single penny of taxes on that profit; and/or (2) shield $125,000 worth of their profit from the IRS if they meet certain rules.

In sum, if you sincerely want to be rich (or just richer),

becoming a homeowner is a pretty sure way to accomplish just that.

True, tax reform has cut back the blessings of homeownership a bit—indirectly.

With tax rates going down, the deductions for property taxes and for mortgage payments aren't worth as much as they used to be. If you were in the 38.5 percent tax bracket in 1987, every additional $100 you paid for any deductible expenses wound up costing you merely $61.50. (You could deduct $38.50 from your taxable income if you itemized.) In 1988, if you're in the 28 percent bracket, a deductible $100 expense will cost you $72, not just $61.50.

Then too, the lenient treatment of long-term capital gains has flown out the window (long-term: over six months). In 1986, you had to pay taxes on only 40 percent of your long-term gains. In 1987, you wouldn't have to pay more than a 28 percent rate on your gains, even if you were in the 38.5 percent bracket. In 1988, long-term capital gains are being taxed like your salary and other "ordinary" income— perhaps as high as 33 percent. That means homeowners who can't shield their capital gains from taxes will be socked harder than they were in the past. (Hence the rush people were in to sell their houses at the end of 1986.)

But some deductions are better than no deductions. And those twin blessings bestowed upon homeowners—tax deferral and the onetime $125,000 exclusion—are therefore now worth far more than ever.

Clearly, being a homeowner—before and AFTER tax reform—is being on the good side of Uncle Sam.

If you're young, as a general rule, you should save up to buy a house—or a condo or coop or mobile home. If you're already a homeowner, as a general rule, remain a homeowner.

Of course, don't buy a house if you can't really afford it—if your job is insecure, or if you'll strip yourself bare of emergency money by making a down payment. And don't buy the wrong house in the wrong area. But for all sorts of reasons besides tax reasons, DO try to buy a house.

263 BUY A HOUSE THIS YEAR.

You can begin deducting your property taxes and mortgage interest THIS year if you buy a house now rather than waiting. Remember the cardinal rule of tax avoidance: Defer income, and take deductions now.

You can also deduct any points you might pay to obtain your mortgage. Points are special charges lenders may levy to lower the interest rate on your mortgage. Each point equals 1 percent of your loan. If you take out a $50,000 mortgage and must pay three points, it's $1,500. You can deduct these points all at once in the year you pay them if (a) you obtain a new mortgage (you don't refinance your old one), and (b) you pay the charges up front, all at once—you don't add the charges to your mortgage balance, paying them off over the life of your loan. You must also segregate money you pay for points from other closing costs, like title insurance. Use a separate check. ("Closing" refers to transactions during the final sale of real estate.)

Of course, there may be good reasons for you NOT to buy a house this year. You might have more money for a down payment next year, and thus be able to wangle a mortgage at a lower interest rate by making a more hefty down payment. Or you want to make sure that your job is stable, or you think your local housing market is too high and prices might plummet. But other things being equal, buy a house this year rather than next.

264 CONSIDER A HOME-EQUITY LOAN.

To hear lenders tell it, the home equity line of credit is just about the most wonderful innovation since double-entry bookkeeping. But to hear consumer advocates talk, the home-equity line of credit is more akin to the invention of debtors' prisons.

The truth lies somewhere in between. Such loans can be a blessing for the sophisticated, and—for the unsophisticated—the equivalent of a loaded pistol in the hands of a temperamental child.

First, some basics.

A home-equity line of credit is a variety of second mortgage. It's a loan backed by the value of your free-and-clear ownership (equity) in your first or second home. Typically you can borrow up to 75 percent of that equity. So, if your house is worth $100,000 and the outstanding balance of your first mortgage is $20,000, you could borrow up to $55,000 ($100,000 times 75 percent minus $20,000).

If, instead of a line of credit, you were to get a $55,000 second mortgage, you'd receive a lump sum and begin paying interest on the total amount. But with a line of credit, you can borrow up to $55,000 at any time. If you withdrew $5,000, you'd pay interest only on that $5,000—and the remaining $55,000 would remain available.

Home-equity lines of credit thus cost you less: You don't pay interest except on the amount you borrow. Other advantages:

A. MUCH OF THE INTEREST YOU PAY MAY BE DEDUCTIBLE. The Tax Reform Act of 1986 started lowering the boom on interest you can deduct for "consumer" debt—car payments, credit card loans, and so forth. You can deduct only 65 percent for 1987, 40 percent for 1988, 20 percent for 1989, 10 percent for 1990, and zilch after that.

But you can still fully deduct the interest you pay on loans secured by your first or second residences—up to the original purchase price of your residence plus the cost of improvements. (If you obtained a mortgage before August 16, 1986, there's no limit on what's deductible.)

This means that if you were planning to borrow to pay for something expensive—a boat, a vacation trip—you can now obtain a home-equity line of credit and magically make all of THAT interest deductible, so long as you're not spending money borrowed against the appreciation of your house.

You can also deduct interest on mortgage loans to pay medical expenses, educational costs, or home improvements—BEYOND the purchase price plus improvements and INCLUDING the appreciated value of your house.

So if you were planning to borrow to pay for medical or educational expenses, you can get a home-equity line of credit and deduct all of the interest—instead of a diminishing percentage. All the interest for traditionally deductible medical expenses remains deductible (except if used to buy health insurance). And you can deduct loan interest for educational expenses BEYOND what has traditionally been deductible (expenses to "maintain or improve" your current job skills). Now you're allowed to deduct interest for loans for primary, secondary, college, or graduate school tuition, along with books, student fees, and supplies. And if you or your dependents live away from home to attend school, you can also deduct interest on loans to pay your living costs.

Yet these potential tax benefits shouldn't sweep you off your feet. Reasons:

• High closing costs (for an appraisal, legal fees, and so forth) can easily wipe out any tax savings on a small home-equity line of credit.

• Tax-wise, you may be better off getting a loan a few years down the road, when less consumer interest is deductible.

• Finally, with tax rates shrinking, deductions in general aren't as valuable now.

In short, you'll have to do some figuring to make sure the tax benefits of such a loan are worthwhile.

B. THE TERMS CAN BE ATTRACTIVE. Because competition among lenders is fierce now, you may be able to swing a home-equity line of credit with no closing costs at all, or modest ones—$250, say, for a $20,000 loan. (Generally, 1.25 percent of the loan is standard.)

Besides, right now the interest rate on such loans is reasonable—usually one to two points above prime (the lowest rate a lender charges its most reliable business customers). The line of credit rate is currently 9–10 percent. If you're paying 17–18 percent interest on credit cards, or 14 percent on personal loans, both of which are only partly deductible, why not pay 10 percent, fully deductible, on a home-equity line of credit?

Again, a few provisos:

• A straightforward second mortgage may be better if you need a lump sum for, say, a home improvement, and not continuing loans for, say, tuition payments. While closing costs may be higher with a second mortgage, you're more likely to wangle a fixed rate of interest. Lines of credit usually carry a variable rate, floating with the prime, and with no cap, or limit, on how much the rate can rise.

• Refinancing your first mortgage may also be better. You'll probably pay a lower interest rate, get a longer term (up to thirty years, whereas a typical line of credit may come due in five or ten years), and more money as well (80 percent of a house's value should be a breeze). If your first mortgage is at a relatively high rate, you're probably FAR better off refinancing.

C. YOU MAY HAVE A GOOD REASON TO BORROW. Prudent homeowners might encounter an investment opportunity that, taken at the flood, will lead to fortune. Or they may want to launch their own well-planned businesses, send themselves to graduate school, or bring their nineteenth-century kitchens into the late twentieth century.

Summing up the argument for home-equity lines of credit, Michael G. Noah, a vice president of Goldome, the largest mutual-savings bank in the country, says: "Anyone who's a prudent borrower should have one. They're really neat things for the sophisticated. And homeowners do tend to know where they're coming from."

Now the arguments AGAINST home-equity lines of credit:

A. YOU COULD LOSE YOUR HOUSE. If you default on credit card charges, Visa or MasterCard is unlikely to compel you to sell your house at public auction. Most states protect all of your home, or a percentage, against creditors. If you default on paying off a car, the bank that financed it will just take it back. But you COULD lose your home by defaulting on a line-of-credit loan, and that could happen if you lose your job, become ill, or separate from your spouse.

"Your house doesn't make the payments," notes Robert J. Hobbs, staff lawyer with the National Consumer Law Center in Boston. "YOU make the payments. And if your income declines, you could be in big trouble."

True, foreclosures as a result of home-equity lines of credit have been rare. But this may be largely due to the fact that such loans have become popular only in the past few years.

In one recent month, reports Mel R. Stiller, executive director of the Consumer Credit Counseling Service of Eastern Massachusetts, four people came to his office because of difficulty repaying such loans. They were the first he had seen. "They were all white-collar types—professionals," he adds, and all had obtained the loans for seemingly sensible reasons: home improvements, investments, education, consolidating debts.

Stiller notes that, in the past, homeowners composed 37–38 percent of his agency's clients. Now they make up only 13 percent. He's afraid that, instead of seeking credit help when they need it, homeowners are using home-equity lines of credit to bail themselves out—like people who take aspirin to combat pain, and postpone seeing a physician until they are seriously ill. This suggests that difficulty repaying home-equity lines of credit may become epidemic. (Stiller himself maintains that such loans "can be a good product for the right people and the right reasons.")

B. SOME PEOPLE WILL ABUSE THEIR LOANS. Most Americans, if they were to obtain such loans, would do it to consolidate their debts, according to a recent Harris poll. This seems to be a worthy purpose. But if people have gone haywire with charge accounts and credit cards, it's not improbable that they will go haywire with home-equity lines of credit, particularly the kind that come with credit cards.

Getting too much money too soon is dangerous enough. It's even worse when it's "funny money." There's less pain in writing a check than paying cash, less pain in using a credit card than writing a check.

The fundamental danger is that homeowners will not recognize the wisdom of letting the money supposedly "locked" in their homes just sit there quietly appreciating—instead of threatening it by means of an ill-considered loan.

Few investments are as solid as real estate. It appreciates nicely in normal times, spectacularly in inflationary times. Your equity in your home also serves as a cushion against emergencies. If you pay off your mortgage, you can probably afford to remain in your old homestead when you retire, or you can trade down to a smaller house in the area, using your profit to bolster your retirement funds.

But you may not be able to retire WHEN you want to, or WHERE you want to, if you're still paying off mortgages or if you have scant equity in your home.

265 GET THE BEST HOME-EQUITY LOAN AVAILABLE.

Look for

• no fees of any kind—no closing costs and no bank charges

• a fixed rate of interest (You'll know what to expect from month to month.)

• next best, a variable interest rate, but with caps on how high the rate can go, and how fast

• a requirement that the borrower immediately begin repaying principal (Otherwise, you may stall and stall—and owe more and more.)

• no prepayment penalty (If you don't have a fixed-rate loan, you may want to pay off the balance if interest rates suddenly rise—and you won't want to be hit by an extra charge.)

• no ongoing fees—such as charges for checks, or a penalty for not using the credit that's available, or fees for "general administration"

If your lender doesn't offer a credit card attached to the home-equity loan, it may be a sign that the lender is responsible, and doesn't want borrowers using the money for frivolous reasons.

266 GET ONE ONLY FOR A SPECIFIC PURPOSE.

Here's a true tale that may imbue in your mind the danger of home-equity lines of credit:

A few years ago, Stephen Del Grosso, thirty-five, seemed to have everything—a $200,000 house near Boston, a $12,000 time-share on Cape Cod, an ample wine cellar, two new cars, a big-screen TV, $1,500 worth of photographic equipment, and more. He and his wife dined frequently at the best ($150 a meal) restaurants. His income as a computer salesman was $91,000; his wife's, as an office administrator, was $20,000.

What he DIDN'T have was a home-equity line of credit. When he took out one, it proved his undoing.

He had decided to obtain the loan to turn his basement into a recreation room and to upgrade his gravel driveway, at a cost of $15,000 to $20,000. The trouble was that the $40,000 line of credit he got "lulled me into a false sense of wealth. I thought of my card as a Gold MasterCard, with $40,000 I could do with as I wished." For example, he also bought his wife a belated diamond wedding ring, for $12,000. "She deserved it," he says. "But I also managed to use up $24,000 in the blink of an eye."

And then his family income nose-dived.

Not realizing the debt load he was carrying, Del Grosso took a job with a new computer company, hoping for a piece of the action. His guaranteed salary was $45,000; with all the start-up work he had to do, he earned no sales commissions at all. Unexpectedly, his wife became pregnant (they already had a three-year-old) and left her job. Their family income went from $110,000 a year to $45,000. His debt load from mortgages and credit-card loans amounted to $4,400 a month, $52,800 a year.

To pay off his new debts, he used his home-equity card—and that just added to his burden. "It was a vicious circle."

He fell three months behind on his first mortgage and behind on his other debts as well. Creditors hounded him day and night. "It was terrible. Someone phoned and demanded $150. I said, 'I have $2.00 in my pocket. Should I mortgage my child?'" Friction developed in his marriage.

In desperation Del Grosso turned to a credit counseling service, and for the first time learned the extent of his debts—and how little income he had to pay for them. But the service persuaded his creditors to allow him to pay only interest, not principal, for a while.

Today the Del Grossos rarely eat out, and if they do, they spend $12 on a Chinese meal. They are preparing to sell their time-share. They have stopped buying new cars, new clothes, and new furniture. Their wine cellar is neglected, their basement remains a basement.

Del Grosso expects that commissions from selling computers will soon pour in, enabling him to make his debts more manageable. Meanwhile, he has advice for others considering home-equity lines of credit: ''Get one for a specific purpose, and use it only for that specific purpose. Don't let it lull you into a false sense of unlimited wealth.''

267 REMAIN IN A HOME YOU OWN.

Once you leave, for an apartment or another residence you don't own, you may owe taxes on any profits you've made from selling your home. So, apart from the fact that most people prefer living in their own homes, for tax reasons try to live in residences that you yourself own. And try not to move often. If you move every few years, closing costs will cut down, if not cancel out, your gains.

When you and your spouse die, your heirs will inherit the house without ever having to pay taxes on the capital gains your house (or houses) have garnered over the years. (Death may be inevitable, but obviously that's not always true of taxes.) The other two chief ways of reducing or eliminating capital-gains taxes on the sale of your residence follow.

268 ROLL OVER YOUR GAINS.

You can postpone (at least) paying taxes on the appreciation of your house when you sell it if

a. you buy and live in another main home within two years after (or before) selling your old one. Yes, you can qualify even if you buy (or build) a new main home two years before selling your old one.

b. the new home is as expensive as or more expensive than the old one.

c. the homes you sold and bought are your main residences (not your summer homes). You could, of course, buy a second home in a resort area, use it as a vacation

home for two years, THEN make it your main residence
when you sell your other home.

You can use this deferral tactic over and over. But you
cannot use it more than once every two years—unless you
move because of a job change and you fulfill the requirements to deduct the expenses on your tax return if you
itemized your deductions.

The postponement of these taxes could come back to
haunt you, though. The basis of (total investment in) your
NEW house is lowered by whatever amount you avoided
paying taxes on. If you avoided paying taxes on $20,000 of
capital gains, then bought a $100,000 house, its basis would
be only $80,000. That means that someday—when you sell
that $100,000 house—you might have to pay taxes on that
$20,000 profit. But you may be in a lower tax bracket when
that day comes—and you'll have had all that extra time to
use the money as you see fit. But remember: If you die
while living in your main residence, the IRS will ignore all
those capital gains.

What if you don't need a bigger house? How can you still
buy a house at least as expensive and thus defer paying taxes
on your gain? Buy a smaller house—but in a more expensive area. Or add improvements within two years of selling
your old house, to bring the cost of your new house up to
the sales price of your old one. Many people sell their
homes when their kids move out, and buy a smaller place—
but with larger grounds, just to have a more expensive house
for tax purposes.

If your main house is a trailer, houseboat, or yacht, it still
qualifies for the deferral tactic—whether it's your old or your
new residence. And your replacement residence doesn't even
have to be in this country. In fact, if your home is outside
the country—because, say, you're in the armed forces—you
may have longer than two years to buy or build a replacement home.

269 CHOOSE WHICH GAIN TO PAY TAXES ON.

You may have a choice. Let's say that you sell your house for $100,000. You have a $20,000 gain. You buy another house for $90,000. Do you owe taxes on the $20,000 gain—or on the $10,000 that cannot be deferred? The IRS lets you choose the lower amount—in this case, the $10,000 is subtracted from the $90,000 to become the tax basis of your new house—$80,000.

270 BOOST YOUR HOUSE'S BASIS.

The higher your house's basis, the less capital gains there will be that might be taxed—if you ever are required to pay those taxes. Here's what you can add to your purchase price:

• closing costs, such as legal fees, recorder's fees, title insurance, and a termite inspection
• the cost of improvements. Examples are a new furnace, new carpeting, a new fence, central air conditioning, new wiring or new plumbing. Repairs—such as patching your roof, or having a leaky pipe fixed—don't qualify. But REPLACING your roof does. You can use the original cost of your improvements—even if you tacked down that carpeting years ago and it's rather tacky now. Don't count your own labor as part of the cost of an improvement. (This is a good argument for letting someone else do it.)
• legal expenses connected with any improvements—such as your hiring a lawyer to get a variance (an exception to the planning code) so you can add an extra room
• a real-estate agent's fee, if you as a buyer used an agent (which seems to be growing more common)
• the cost of appliances you bought and left with the purchaser of your house, so long as you didn't sell them

separately from the house (room air conditioners, stove, microwave, and so forth)

• assessments for local improvements, like new sidewalks or the widening of streets

By the same token, you must lower your basis by casualty losses that you deducted in previous years (like the cost of a living room that was destroyed by fire); by residential energy credits you took (remember them?); and, of course, by any gains deferred from sales of your other houses.

271 DON'T FORGET ANY IMPROVEMENTS.

You won't overlook major items like an addition to your house, a new deck, or central air-conditioning. But don't forget new shelves, a repaved or widened driveway, new plants and bushes, wallpapering a room that had been painted. Inspect your property, inside and outside, to refresh your memory.

272 ADD TO YOUR BASIS EVEN IF YOU DON'T HAVE RECEIPTS.

Ideally, you'll have kept all your canceled checks, credit-card chits, and sales slips. If not, you may be able to get away with producing building permits for improvements, property-tax records, or before-and-after photographs of your house.

273 CONSIDER A HOME-IMPROVEMENT LOAN.

If you obtain such a loan, backed by your equity in your house, you can deduct the interest, in full. (The best bets, as far as getting a good return on your investment: a good new kitchen; anything that brings your house up to the level of houses around you—for example, adding a third bedroom if houses around you have three or more; and remedying any defects your house has—not enough bathrooms, for instance.) Such improvements should add a good chunk to the value of your house. And if you must someday pay a capital-gains tax on the house's profits, you can add the cost of your improvements to the house price, thus reducing your tax. Meanwhile, of course, your house will have been more pleasurable to live in.

274 REDUCE YOUR GAIN WITH MOVING EXPENSES YOU COULDN'T DEDUCT.

You're better off itemizing your moving expenses, to get your deductions sooner (see Chapter 3). But if you can't itemize (because the sum of your deductions doesn't exceed the standard deduction), or you've reached the limits on your deductible moving expenses, add whatever expenses you can to the basis of your house or to the adjusted sales price. For example, reduce the basis of your new home by a real-estate agent's commission you paid.

275 LOWER YOUR TAXABLE SALES PRICE.

By lowering your sales price for tax purposes, your gain will again be lower. Here's what you can subtract to wind up with your "adjusted sales price":

* real-estate agent's commissions
* legal fees, geological surveys, maps, termite inspections, and so forth
* any loan charges, such as points, that you as the seller must pay (if your buyer obtained, for example, a Veterans Administration–backed mortgage)
* the cost of advertising, for-sale signs, and fact sheets if

you sold your house yourself, without benefit of a broker (You can deduct them even if you wound up having a broker sell your house.)

• fix-up expenses for work performed during the ninety days before you sold your home, and paid for within thirty days after the sale. (The narrow time-limit is to ensure that the expenses were truly to help you sell the house.) Examples: the cost of having the exterior or interior of your house painted, your plumbing repaired, new wallpaper installed. You can deduct fix-up costs only if you buy a less expensive house—because if you buy a house as expensive, you must defer the gains. The fix-up costs would then serve to boost the basis of your new house.

Here's an example of all these calculations, provided by the IRS: Your selling expenses were $5,000. You spent $900 on new blinds and on a new water heater; you also spent $800 on painting your house—and met the rules regarding such fix-up expenses.

1. Selling price of old home: $61,400
2. Selling expenses: $5,000
3. Amount realized (1 minus 2): $56,400
4. Basis of old home: $45,000
5. Improvements (blinds, heater): $900
6. New basis of home (4 plus 5): $45,900
7. Gain on old home (3 minus 6): $10,500

You buy and live in another home costing $54,600 within two years of selling your old one. Now you can defer paying taxes on most of that $10,500.

8. Amount realized: $56,400
9. Fix-up expenses (painting): $800
10. Adjusted sales price (8 minus 9): $55,600
11. Cost of replacement home: $54,600
12. Gain NOT postponed (10 minus 11): $1,000

13. Gain postponed (7 minus 12): $9,500
14. Cost of new home: $54,600
15. Adjusted basis of new home (14 minus 13): $45,000

276   DEDUCT A LOSS ON SELLING YOUR HOUSE . . .

if you were renting it out. Some homeowners who are selling for losses—typically because they bought a home in a deteriorating neighborhood, or where the main industry left—rent their houses for a few months, then try to deduct their loss. No good. You must prove to the IRS that you were renting the house for a profit, not just to deduct the loss on its sale. The longer you were renting it out, the more persuasive a case you can make. And you may need appraisals showing that the house had NOT declined in value before you began renting it out.

277   TAKE THE $125,000 EXCLUSION.

You can subtract $125,000 from your gain if (a) your house was your main residence, (b) you or your spouse were fifty-five when you sold the house (you didn't turn fifty-five at the end of that year) and owned it jointly, and (c) you or your spouse lived there for three of the five years before you sold it.

You can use this exclusion just once in your lifetime. But you can undo a mistake. Let's say that you use the exclusion to escape taxes on $20,000 of gain. You buy another house, and a few years later, you sell that one, for a $50,000 gain. You have three years from the date that your earlier return (with the smaller $20,000 exclusion) was due to be filed to cancel that first exclusion.

278   TAKE THE EXCLUSION EVEN IF YOUR QUALIFYING SPOUSE DIED.

If you and your spouse owned the house jointly, and your spouse was fifty-five or older, and had lived there for three of the past five years, you qualify for the exclusion—even if you're not fifty-five, or hadn't lived in the house for three of the past five years.

279 CONSIDER THE EXCLUSION WHEN YOU MARRY.

Let's say you've never used the exclusion, and you're living in your own house. Now you plan to marry someone who HAS used the exclusion before, and you plan to live in your house when you marry. You'll be better off selling your house before you marry. The fact that your new spouse had used the $125,000 exclusion would keep YOU from being able to use it—or even half of it.

280 TAKE THE EXCLUSION EVEN IF YOU RENTED OUT THE HOUSE.

You qualify if you rented the house for two years, and lived there the previous three years.

281 CHOOSE DEFERRAL OVER THE EXCLUSION.

By and large, the deferral tactic is better. You can use it again and again. And at a later time in your life, the exclusion may be more suitable—because you may want to live in a small house, or in an apartment. Also, your taxable gain may be higher later in life, because of the lowered basis of your last house, the result of all those deferrals.

282 TAKE BOTH.

Consider taking all of the $125,000 exclusion, AND deferring the tax you owe on your remaining profit.

Here's an example, from the accounting firm of Seidman & Seidman/BDO:

You're fifty-five, and sell your primary residence for $400,000 (Seidman & Seidman must have well-to-do clients!). The basis of your residence was $75,000.

1. Sales price of old home: $400,000
2. Tax basis of old home: $75,000
3. Gain (1 minus 2): $325,000
4. Exclusion: $125,000
5. Taxable gain (3 minus 4): $200,000

Now let's say that you buy a new house for $300,000. And now you can invoke the deferral tactic—even though your new house costs far less than your old one!

6. Sales price: $400,000
7. Exclusion: $125,000
8. New sales price (6 minus 7): $275,000
9. Price of new home: $300,000
10. Taxable gain (8 minus 9): 0
11. Tax basis of new home (9 minus 5): $100,000

283 REFINANCE YOUR MORTGAGE.

As a rule, if current mortgage interest rates are two points below the rate you're paying now, and you plan on living in your home for at least a few years, it's probably worthwhile to get a new mortgage. First of all, you'll save on mortgage payments. And second, assuming you refinance for more than your current mortgage balance, you will have more money at your disposal (because you will have paid off some of the principal). And the interest on the amount of your new mortgage will be fully deductible, provided that it's less than your house's original purchase price plus the cost of improvements. (I'm assuming you will make good use of that extra money.)

284 OWN YOUR HOUSE JOINTLY.

That way, if you or your spouse dies, the surviving spouse will inherit the house without court probate costs.

285 SELL YOUR HOUSE TO YOUR KIDS.

If you're getting on in years and need the money, sell your house to your children, in return for an annuity—a regular stream of payments for as long as you live. Otherwise, your house will be subject to estate taxes when you die, and your children's inheritance will shrink.

Chapter Eleven
EMPLOYEES

Tax reform has made things a bit difficult for employees. Now, many of their job-related expenses must be listed on Schedule A as "miscellaneous" expenses, instead of being deducted directly from total income. And their total job-related expenses (together with other miscellaneous deductions) must exceed 2 percent of their adjusted gross incomes before they can actually be used as itemized deductions. (Adjusted gross income: total income minus things like deductible contributions to an IRA and alimony you pay.)

Some other changes:

Travel for general educational purposes is no longer deductible. French teachers cannot spend their summers in Paris, absorbing the culture, and deduct their costs. (But see Tip 291.)

Outside salespersons—those who work mainly on the road and at home—must now itemize their expenses, which also must surpass the 2 percent floor. Once upon a time, these expenses were deductible on Form 1040; you didn't have to itemize.

The "two-earner" deduction is no longer available. (It was fun while it lasted.)

An employee can no longer deduct the cost of deducting home-office expenses when the employer leases the office in the employee's home. (Under such an arrangement, the employee could get deductions for a home office without meeting the strict requirements.)

Also, home-office deductions in general are now limited to your income from your at-home business. (But you can carry over any losses to later years.)

286 DON'T INCLUDE REIMBURSE-MENTS IN YOUR INCOME . . .

if they don't exceed your expenses, and if you report your expenses to your employer, via an expense account, petty-cash vouchers, or whatever. Otherwise, you must report reimbursements on Form 2106, or in a statement attached to your return.

If your reimbursements do exceed your expenses, enter the excess as "Other Income"—unless your employer has already included it on your Form W-2.

What if your employer reimburses you for expenses, but you don't give him or her an accounting? You can subtract business expenses your employer pays you for; it's an adjustment to your gross income. But you must report the same reimbursements as income, so it evens out.

"Accounting to your employer" means that you give him or her an expense account or other written statement showing the business nature and amounts of your expenses, broken down into broad categories like transportation, meals and lodging while away from home overnight, and entertainment.

287 PUSH YOUR EMPLOYEE-RELATED EXPENSES INTO ONE YEAR.

To jump over the 2 percent floor, try to have a banner year as far as your nonreimbursed deductible employee expenses are concerned. Such expenses include:

• business phone calls from your home that your employer doesn't cover

- subscriptions to business publications
- educational expenses (see below)
- expenses for searching for a new job in your same line of work, even if you don't get the job or you turn it down
- dues for your union or professional association
- work clothes, required for your job, that you wouldn't wear off the job
- 80 percent of entertainment expenses (taking a client to a ball game)
- legal expenses for negotiating an employment contract
- the cost of small tools and supplies
- the cost of periodical health exams required by your employer

Here's an example of how to "bunch" your deductions: In the same year that you'll have deductible educational expenses, buy new equipment for your home office.

288 REMEMBER EXPENSES THAT AREN'T SUBJECT TO THE 2-PERCENT RULE.

These are worth more. Among them: moving expenses (see Chapter 3); the special work expenses of a handicapped person (typically, the cost of an attendant); the expenses of certain performing artists—those who work for at least two employers in the performing arts during the year, whose expenses exceed 10 percent of their wages, and whose adjusted gross incomes (before these expenses) are not over $16,000. (President Reagan, as you know, is a former performing artist—which may explain this tax break.)

289 DEDUCT MORE THAN THE COST OF A PHONE CALL.

As part of your job, you regularly phone clients while you're working at home. Your employer doesn't reimburse you—

"Your salary is so high, it should cover it," he or she says unsympathetically. Deduct not just the cost of the phone calls. Also deduct the 3 percent excise tax on each call, and deduct the cost of having the phone in your home to begin with—according to a ratio of how much you use the phone for yourself and for your business.

290 DON'T DEDUCT THE COST OF YOUR BRIEFCASE.

Why not? Because, a shrewd accountant once told me, IRS agents probably don't deduct the cost of THEIR briefcases, and you might tick them off if they examine your return.

291 DEDUCT TRAVEL EXPENSES FOR STUDY OR RESEARCH.

If you travel for a specific purpose, you may still be able to deduct your expenses—if your employer doesn't cover their cost. An economics teacher could go to the London School of Economics to take a course not available elsewhere, or read rare books at the British Museum for a new course he or she is teaching, and deduct the travel expenses—so long as the other expenses (the courses, meals, lodgings) also qualify as deductible.

You must subtract 20 percent from the cost of meals and entertainment. And all the expenses must exceed 2 percent of your adjusted gross income to be deductible.

292 DEDUCT EDUCATIONAL EXPENSES TO PROTECT YOUR JOB.

Normally, you can deduct educational expenses if they maintain or improve your skills in your job. But you can also deduct such expenses if they are needed to keep you from losing your current job benefits. A teacher was allowed to claim the cost of courses she took only to qualify for annual salary increases.

293 TAKE CLASSES IN 1987.

In 1987, any payments your employer makes for courses you take will be tax-free, up to $5,250. In 1988 and in later years, reimbursed tuition costs may be partially taxable.

294 INCLUDE TRANSPORTATION COSTS.

If your educational courses are deductible, so are the transportation costs to and fro. If you go home after work, before going to school, deduct the cost only to the extent it doesn't exceed the cost of your going directly from work to school.

295 CONSIDER DEDUCTING THEATER TICKETS AS "ENTERTAINMENT."

You give theater or sports-event tickets to a business associate. You could list it as a gift, but a gift is limited to a deduction of $25 per person. You may be better off listing it as an entertainment expense, which has no limits. But remember that entertainment expenses have a 20 percent bite taken out before they're deductible. If the tickets are inexpensive, they may be better taken as a gift.

296 USE THE COST OF A SINGLE ROOM ...

if you took your spouse along on a business trip. Don't deduct half the cost of a double room. A single might cost $60, a double $75. Go for $60, not half of $75 ($37.50).

297 DON'T OVERLOOK SMALL TRAVEL EXPENSES.

Examples: the cost of dry cleaning and laundry, tips, baggage charges, phone calls home. You won't forget such major expenses as transportation, food, and lodgings.

Travel expenses are those you incur outside the metropolitan area where you work, and if you remain overnight—or at least long enough to need some rest before you return.

298 DEDUCT COMMUTING COSTS . . .

if you must travel from one place to another for the same employer, or for different employers. You can deduct only the cost of going from one place of work to another—not the cost of leaving and returning home. For example, a doctor can deduct the cost of traveling to various hospitals to visit patients.

Normal commuting expenses are not deductible.

299 DEDUCT FOR THE COST OF YOUR SPOUSE . . .

if you entertain a business customer, and his or her spouse joins you. It would be awkward if you DIDN'T bring your own spouse. So it's an "ordinary and necessary" business expense.

300 DEDUCT FOR DUES PAID TO KIWANIS, LIONS, ROTARY, OR OTHER BUSINESS CLUBS.

They're deductible if they qualify as ordinary and necessary business expenses, as they normally do. You can also deduct dues paid to legal, medical, or other professional associations.

As for dues to country clubs, golf clubs, and so forth, you must use such clubs more than 50 percent of the time to help you in your business, and—if you do—you can deduct only the portion of your dues directly related to your business.

301   HAVE A GOOD EXCUSE FOR EXPENSIVE MEALS.

The IRA won't allow any deduction for "lavish and extravagant" meals, but doesn't explain what those terms mean. If you take someone out for an expensive meal, be sure you can explain why you incurred the expense. Perhaps the person was an important client, thinking about throwing a lot of business your way.

Keep good records for all entertainment and meals. The old rule: You must record the time, place, and the cost of the meal, and the name of the businessperson you ate with. Now you must also record the specific business transacted, or the topic of business conversation that took place during the meal.

If your employer doesn't pay you directly for business expenses, ask your employer to start—so you won't have to itemize and surpass the floor of 2 percent of your adjusted gross income before you get any of your money back.

302   DEDUCT FOR WORK CLOTHES...

if they're required for your job and you can't normally wear them outside the office. Also deduct for the cost of safety equipment like goggles and hard hats. People who can deduct the cost of work clothes include athletes, fire fighters, transportation employees (bus drivers, airplane pilots), police officers, letter carriers, nurses, entertainers, civilian teachers in a military school. A painter deducted the white overalls his employer required; surgeons have deducted surgical smocks; a car repairman deducted high-top shoes, jumpers, and leather-palm gloves; an art teacher deducted the cost of protective smocks.

303 DEDUCT FOR HAVING THEM CLEANED . . .

if it's a question of safety (you work around machinery, and baggy clothes might get entangled).

304 CLAIM A HOME OFFICE.

Don't be afraid of claiming a home office—if it's for the convenience of your employer. The rules are strict, but if you qualify, you can save a sizable chunk of taxes.

The rules: Your office at home must be used as (a) your main place of business (it can be a sideline business), or (b) as a place of business used by your customers in meeting with you. You must use a portion of your residence regularly and exclusively for either (a) or (b).

The home office must be "separately identifiable," though it needn't be separated from the rest of a room by dividers or curtains.

Your deductions generally should be based on the space your office occupies compared with the rest of your home—for example, one-tenth.

While tax reform has limited your deductions to your net home-office income, you can carry forward your tax losses to future years, to offset income from your home business.

305 DON'T OVERLOOK DEDUCTIBLE HOME-OFFICE EXPENSES.

You can deduct a portion of many home expenses, such as having your driveway sealed, the central air-conditioning repaired, the cost of a cleaning person, and having the outside painted. Normal expenses are gas, electricity, water, insurance, depreciation, rent. DON'T deduct for lawn care—the IRS specifically excludes it. If you deduct local taxes or mortgage interest, you'll have to subtract those expenses from the overall local taxes and mortgage interest you deduct.

306 STOP DEDUCTING YOUR HOME OFFICE THE YEAR BEFORE YOU SELL.

Otherwise, the profit from the portion of your home you used for an office will not qualify for the deferral option or the $125,000 exclusion.

307 DEDUCT FOR A HOME COMPUTER.

You can use the Section 179 ("expensing") deduction to write off the cost—up to $10,000—in one year. Be prepared to prove that the computer was used more than 50 percent of the time for business. Either you must use the computer for your own business reasons (to manage your investments, for example), or because your employer requires you to have one.

308 DECIDE WHICH IS BETTER— ACTUAL CAR EXPENSES OR THE STANDARD RATE.

You have a choice: Either deduct actual expenses, or deduct a standard mileage rate. The second has the advantage of less record keeping. But use Form 2106, to work it out both ways, and see which saves you more money.

The actual expenses way: Deduct for owning and operating costs, including insurance, repairs, taxes and licenses, loan interest, garage rent, parking fees and tolls, depreciation, gasoline and oil.

If you use the car partly for business and partly for personal driving, apportion the expenses. If you drive 10,000 miles a year to visit customers, and 5,000 for shopping, social, and vacation trips, you can deduct two-thirds of your expenses.

The standard-mileage rate: Deduct 21 cents a mile for the first 15,000 miles of business use, 11 cents a mile above that.

Even when you use the standard-mileage rate, you can deduct parking fees and tolls, state and local taxes, and loan interest (for the business use of the car).

The new depreciation rules (and every year there seem to be new rules): A car put in use must be depreciated over five years, not just three. During the first year, you can deduct the lesser of $2,250 or 20 percent of the cost; second year, $4,100 or 32 percent; third year, $2,450 or 19.2 percent; fourth year, $1,475 or 11.5 percent; fifth year, $1,475 or 11.5 percent. After that, any value left in the car can't be depreciated at more than $1,475 a year. Naturally, you'll reduce the depreciation you take by the percentage of your personal use of the car.

If your business use of the car is 50 percent or less, use straight-line depreciation, not accelerated.

Luxury autos—those costing over $12,800—can be written off only over ten years.

309 USE A NEWER CAR FOR BUSINESS.

If you have a choice of two cars to use for business driving, consider choosing the one with less than 60,000 miles on it. That way you can deduct 21 cents a mile, up to 15,000 miles, instead of the 11-cents-a-mile rate required for cars already driven for 60,000 miles or more.

310 KEEP YOUR "LUXURY" CAR FOR PERSONAL USE.

A luxury car is one that costs $12,800, and you can write it off only over ten years. You'll probably get rid of it before then—and lose some depreciation deductions. You can depreciate a less expensive car faster. So consider driving to the seashore in your Mercedes, driving to visit customers in your Hyundai.

311 ASK YOUR EMPLOYER TO PROVIDE YOU WITH A CAR.

Explain that, in order to get reimbursed sometime in the future for your business driving expenses, you'll have to qualify to itemize—and you'll lose 2 percent of your expenses anyway.

Don't do any personal driving with the car, or you'll have to report part of the car's use as income.

Chapter Twelve
ENTREPRENEURS

In all sorts of ways, tax breaks for business people have been cut back. Of course, there's the famous 20 percent subtraction of expenses for meals and entertainment (the "three-martini lunch"). And the "quiet" meal—social chit-chat with a customer—won't cut it anymore; you must talk about specific business matters to get a deduction. Meanwhile, depreciation periods have generally been lengthened.

Even so, business owners still enjoy many valuable breaks—and should take advantage of them to the utmost. Overall, entrepreneurs should by and large follow the same strategy as individual taxpayers: take deductions now, and defer income. And they should fund their own retirement plans to the maximum.

312 TRY TO TURN ITEMIZED DEDUCTIONS INTO BUSINESS EXPENSES.

If you run a small sideline business, all your expenses connected with your business are deductible in full, on Schedule C, "Profit or (Loss) From Business or Profession." But many of your itemized deductions, on Schedule A, will be subject to a floor—2 percent of your adjusted gross income.

179

Scrutinize those expenses you've been planning to treat as itemized deductions; maybe they should be treated as deductions related to your business.

313 CONSIDER TURNING YOUR BUSINESS INTO AN S CORPORATION.

An S corporation can have only thirty-five or fewer shareholders, and must be set up under Subchapter S of the tax code. Such corporations have all sorts of alluring benefits.

The profits of non-S corporations are taxed twice: first to the corporation, then to the shareholders. With an S corporation, income isn't taxed to the business—just to the shareholders. And S corporation profits are taxed at the shareholders' lower rates (a top of 33 percent in 1988), not at the higher rates (34 percent) that corporations in general currently pay.

Another bonus of an S corporation: It's not subject to the dreaded alternative minimum tax. For non-S corporations, the AMT has jumped to 20 percent from 15 percent. (S corporation shareholders, however, may be subject to the AMT.) Still another bonus: The business can remain on the "cash basis." (Corporations with annual sales of over $5 million must use the "accrual" basis, which means income must be recognized when it's earned, not when you actually get it.) If you're on the cash basis, you can more easily defer income into a future year.

But S corporations have drawbacks, too. They may be taxed on their built-in capital gains when they convert. They may have to change their tax year—most S corporations must adopt a December 31 year-end—and this may result in a short tax year, with lots of income and few deductions. There can be problems with state taxes. Check with your adviser before going ahead and switching to an S corporation.

314 TAKE AN IMMEDIATE $10,000 WRITE-OFF.

If you buy equipment for your business, you can take the Section 179 ("expensing") deduction—up to $10,000 in the first year. In the past, you had to decide between the investment tax credit and expensing. Now that the credit has flown out the window, expensing makes even more sense. Don't expense business cars. (The maximum first-year deduction for cars put into use after 1986 is $2,560.) In figuring depreciation, subtract the expensing deduction from the property's basis.

You begin to lose the expensing deduction once you've purchased over $200,000 in new equipment. So try to keep below $200,000 in any year.

315 CARRY OVER ANY EXPENSING YOU HAVEN'T USED.

If your business income is only $9,000, you can carry over $1,000 into the next year, to apply against new equipment. Warnings: You must take the deduction in the year you spend the money—you can't go back and file an amended return. Also, once you make a decision about expensing, describing the property and the part of the purchase price you're writing off, you can't change your mind, decide to expense some other property, and amend your return.

316 USE EXPENSING ON EQUIPMENT YOU MUST DEPRECIATE SLOWLY AND CHOOSE ACCELERATED DEPRECIATION WHERE YOU CAN.

Expense equipment that you must depreciate over seven years, not five years, for example.

You can still take accelerated depreciation on certain business items, like computer equipment, put into use after July 31, 1986. (In fact, you can now depreciate them even faster.) And there's a new argument for accelerated depreciation. Time was when you had to pay higher, ordinary-income taxes on profit from the sale of assets that you had depreciated quickly. But because even long-term capital gains are being taxed like ordinary income now, you're not penalized for taking accelerated depreciation. And, of course, the more money you can temporarily save from taxes, the more you'll have to invest.

317 DEFER CORPORATE INCOME INTO 1988, TAKE DEDUCTIONS IN 1987.

The top corporate tax rate has dropped from 46 percent to 34 percent. The 34 percent rate kicked in on July 1, 1987. Deferring income into 1988 will thus save you taxes—beyond what you normally save by deferring income. Taking deductions earlier will also help. In 1987, try to make the maximum deductible contribution into the company's retirement plan; pay for (or incur, if you're on the accrual basis) deductible expenses, like repairs, before the year's end; make charitable contributions before the year's end, and consider doubling up—making next year's contribution this year; check inventories for possible write-offs.

318 PAY YOUR EMPLOYEES BEFORE THE END OF THE YEAR.

If you're on the cash basis, and pay your employees in January for December, you'll have to wait for the following year to deduct the payments. Make out the final weeks' salary checks early, and pay them before the end of the year.

319 DECIDE THAT YOUR HOBBY IS A BUSINESS.

One reason: 1986 was the last year you could deduct losses from a hobby only if you had made a profit in TWO of the previous five years. Now you must have made a profit in THREE of the previous five years.

Another reason: If you decide that your hobby is a business, you can always deduct losses, year after year.

Finally, you can deduct the cost of business trips. If you were a part-time professional photographer last year (you took pictures at weddings, say), write off the cost of visiting trade shows. If you became a part-time professional coin collector, deduct the cost of attending sales and conventions.

To persuade the IRS that your hobby is now a business, set up books and records, and start a separate checking account.

320 SELL YOUR BUSINESS BEFORE 1989.

If you sell your business, the assets will now be taxed at the corporate level, then on the shareholders' level. But there's an exception for closely held corporations valued at $5 million or less. They can liquidate before December 31, 1988, and avoid the corporate tax. (The stock of a closely held corporation isn't generally sold to the public.)

321 DON'T ASSUME YOUR BUSINESS GENERATES "PASSIVE" INCOME.

Just because your business consists of renting cars or video-cassettes, don't assume that it's a passive activity, and you can't write off losses against active income (wages) or portfolio income (capital gains, interest).

If you "materially" participate in a business, it's not a passive activity. And, by definition, material participation means that you're involved in the "operations" on a "regular, continuous, and substantial" basis. If the business is your main employment, it's a good sign.

Rental businesses that require a lot of work on your part obviously aren't "passive." One clue: There's a lot of turnover (people borrowing and returning videocassettes). Another clue:

Your business does more than just rent things. (A car-rental place, for example, must keep the cars running and well maintained—not just rent cars.)

322 OFFER CASH RATHER THAN STOCK OPTIONS.

With tax rates down and the favorable long-term capital-gains tax vanishing, your employees may prefer cash—especially if it's deferred till next year. And your company doesn't get a tax deduction on stock used to compensate employees.

323 HIRE YOUR SPOUSE.

Your spouse can then set up a deductible $2,000 IRA. You won't have to pay Social Security taxes on his or her income, either (though that may change soon). Pay the going rate, keep regular employment records, and give the spouse legitimate work—not a "no show" job.

324 SPEND MORE THAN $25 ON A DEDUCTIBLE GIFT.

You're limited to deducting $25 a year for business gifts to individuals. But incidental costs—wrapping a gift, insuring it, mailing it, having it engraved—don't count toward the $25 limit. And if you give someone a $25 present, you can also give him or her an item costing less than $4 that has your business name on it (like pencils and pens) without infringing the $25 limit.

325 THINK TWICE BEFORE PAYING A PREMIUM FOR CHOICE TICKETS.

The show is sold out? You'll have to pay a huge markup for tickets? Hesitate. You can deduct only 80 percent of the tickets' face value—and none of the premium.

326 DEDUCT FOR ATTENDING BUSINESS CONVENTIONS.

Don't confuse investment seminars with business meetings. You can no longer deduct the cost of traveling to investment seminars, or a seminar's registration fees. But you can still deduct the travel costs, lodgings, registration fees, 80 percent of meals, and so forth when you attend seminars, meetings, or conventions related to your business.

327 DON'T INCLUDE AS INCOME ORDERS YOU HAVEN'T FILLED.

Even if you're on the accrual basis, you don't have to declare income until a sale is completed. So even if you have the orders on hand and merchandise ready for shipment, you needn't report any income until the merchandise is on the way.

328 DON'T INCLUDE PAYMENTS-IN-ADVANCE IN THIS YEAR'S INCOME.

If you're on the accrual basis, and you receive an advance payment in 1988 for work you'll do in 1989, it's income in 1989. (But if you're on the cash basis, it's 1988 income.)

329 DON'T OVERVALUE YOUR INVENTORY.

The cost of your goods isn't just the invoice price, minus any trade discounts. Also add freight charges or other expenses in getting the merchandise to your place of business.

330 DON'T INCLUDE MERCHANDISE YOU HAVEN'T PAID FOR.

Don't include in your inventory any goods you received in December, but didn't get the bills for until January. If you do, you're needlessly increasing your previous year's income by the cost of the goods. Even if you receive the bills in January, treat them as purchases you made in December. That expense will offset the value of the goods.

331 DEDUCT EVEN PARTIAL BUSINESS BAD DEBTS.

Don't confuse a business bad debt with a personal bad debt, which must be TOTALLY worthless to be deductible.

332 DEDUCT FOR BAD DEBTS AS SOON AS POSSIBLE.

You can take a loss for a bad debt only in the year when the obligation becomes worthless—not in a later year. (But you can amend your return for the earlier year.) So don't put it off. Signs that a debt is worthless: the debtor declared bankruptcy; he or she went out of business; a judgment against the debtor can't be collected. (If you have stock that's worthless, a friendly broker may buy it from you, for a penny, just to establish your loss.)

333 DEDUCT CASUALTY LOSSES IN FULL.

In deducting business property that's stolen or destroyed, you need not subtract $100, then 10 percent of your adjusted gross income, as you must with personal property. Deduct the loss on Schedule C.

334 WHEN IN DOUBT, DECIDE SOMETHING IS A REPAIR.

The difference between repairs and improvements can be narrow, but for business-tax purposes, repairs are better.

Repairs can be deducted in the year they're made. Improvements can only be added to the basis of (total investment in) your property, to shrink the capital gains when you sell.

If there's any doubt, you may want to resolve the matter in your favor.

Here's how the IRS distinguishes between improvements and repairs:

An IMPROVEMENT adds to the value of your property, prolongs its useful life, or adapts it to new uses. Putting a recreation room in an unfinished basement, paneling a den, adding a bathroom or bedroom, putting decorative grillwork on a balcony, putting up a fence, putting in new plumbing or wiring, putting in new cabinets, putting on a new roof, and paving a driveway are examples of improvements.

A REPAIR keeps your property in good operating condition. It does not materially add to the value of your property or substantially prolong its life. Repainting property inside or out, fixing gutters or floors, mending leaks, plastering, and replacing broken windows are examples of repairs.

335 DON'T OVERLOOK ANY BUSINESS EXPENSES.

Some that you might forget: donations to business organizations; payments to nonemployees for research, typing, consulting, and so forth; license fees; postage; education expenses; and lobbying expenses.

Chapter Thirteen
PARENTS AND
THE DIVORCED

No longer can you give stocks, bonds, and money to children under fourteen and have all that wealth grow in value while being taxed at the kids' low rates.

Tax reform mandates that a child's unearned income—interest, dividends, rents, royalties, and so forth—will be taxed (beyond $1,000) at the rate of the parent. If the parents are divorced or separated, it's the rate of the higher-earning parent that counts. Why the special $1,000? The standard deduction provides $500, and $500 is taxed at the child's own tax rate—typically, 15 percent for 1988.

A child's earned income (from his job), though, will always be taxed at the child's rate.

Clifford trusts and other income-shifting devices are also out the window. And the final blow: If you take a child as an exemption, the child cannot claim an exemption for himself or herself.

No, this doesn't mean that you shouldn't begin saving for a child's college education, or just for the child's future well-being, until the kid is fourteen. The rules are stricter, and your options more limited, but you can still do a lot for your child—before and after the child is fourteen.

336 REMEMBER THAT $1,000 A YEAR CAN AMOUNT TO A LOT.

You can give a child a $12,500 certificate of deposit yielding 8 percent—and, the first year, it would provide the child with about $1,000 in income, all taxed at the child's rate.

These days, the typical stock yields 3 percent in dividends. That means a child could have $33,333 in stocks, yielding $1,000.

Of course, these yields would quickly rise over $1,000 after the first year. But the point is that $1,000 in unearned income implies a principal that's not to be sneezed at. So you should consider starting a college-education fund way before a child reaches fourteen.

Keep in mind, too, that $1,000 a year, with half untaxed and half taxed at 15 percent, can grow into a pretty decent piece of change. It would be significantly more than your investing $1,000 a year in your own name, taxed at 15 percent, 28 percent, or 33 percent (the rates in 1988 and after).

337 REMEMBER: A CHILD CAN TAKE MORE THAN THE $500 STANDARD DEDUCTION.

If the child's itemized deductions, relating to unearned income, exceed $500, the child can take the higher figure instead. Such deductions might include custodial fees and investment guidance.

338 CONSIDER GIVING $10,000 A YEAR TO A CHILD.

Why $10,000? Because that's the amount not subject to gift taxes that the giver might otherwise have to pay. If you and your spouse combine on a gift, it can be $20,000 a year, untaxed. And that's $20,000 a year TO EACH CHILD.

You might want to wait until a child is fourteen before beginning to give large amounts—when the earnings will be taxed at the child's rate. And giving $20,000 a year to a child of fourteen means that just the principal will be $80,000 when the child is eighteen and about to jaunt off to college. At 10 percent interest, the child would have around $102,000. That should help defray a few expenses.

There's another reason, of course, to give away assets to a child: so the assets won't be taxed as part of your estate when you die.

339 SET UP A CUSTODIAL ACCOUNT.

It's a snap. Just visit or write to a bank, brokerage firm, or mutual fund. You can put cash, stocks, bonds, or other income-producing assets into a custodial account.

Ideally, the custodian won't be a parent but a trusted friend or relative; otherwise, if the parent who made the gift and who serves as custodian dies before the child reaches legal adulthood, the account may be included in the parent's gross estate for estate-tax purposes.

The child will assume control of the account when he or she reaches eighteen or twenty-one, depending on state law.

If you use the account to cover expenses you're legally obligated to pay for—a child's food, medical expenses, and clothing, for instance—the account's income to that extent will be taxed to the parent. In some states, a wealthy parent is required to pay for a child's education—which means that you, as custodian, couldn't use the money for college expenses without owing taxes. But if children reach legal adulthood at eighteen, just when they are entering college, they themselves can use the money to pay for their college expenses. And in most states, eighteen is the legal age of adulthood.

340 CONSIDER GROWTH STOCKS.

One advantage of giving a child stocks is that no taxes need be paid on the stocks' appreciation until you sell them. So, if you put stocks into a child's name, the appreciation can build up—untaxed—year after year.

True, stocks do pay taxable dividends. But small-company or growth stocks pay little if any, and over the years, growth stocks have fared better than blue chips (stocks of older, bigger companies). You might be best off buying a child shares of a mutual fund that specializes in growth stocks. The fund will sell some of them over the years, triggering taxable gains (or deductible losses). But perhaps the fund's improved performance—thanks to its buying and selling—will offset the taxes your child will have to pay on the distributions.

Warning: The stock market can, and has, gone down and stayed there. In 1972–1974, stocks lost almost 50 percent of their value. But stock-market declines rarely have lasted for more than four years. So, if you buy stocks for a very young child, intending to cover his or her college education, you can start selling them when the child is fourteen, fifteen, sixteen, seventeen, or eighteen. During at least one of those years, the market should be high. (For novice investors: Try to sell into a rising market, buy into a declining market.) And once children are nearing college age, and their unearned income is taxed at their own rates, you might put their holdings into very safe, stable investments—like short-term bonds, money-market funds, or certificates of deposit.

If you're thinking of stock mutual funds for a child, look for those with no or low sales charges; low turnover of stocks; and, above all, excellent long-term records.

341 GIVE A CHILD STOCK IN YOUR COMPANY.

If your family owns a company, give your children stock—$10,000 or $20,000 a year, so you won't be subject to gift taxes. If the stock pays no dividends, the child will owe no taxes. When the child reaches fourteen, rebuy the stock. (Or spread out your repurchases over a few years if the child might otherwise wind up in the 28 percent or 33 percent bracket because of high capital gains.)

342 CONSIDER ZERO-COUPON CORPORATE BONDS.

Interest on these bonds (see Chapter 7) accumulates slowly. Annual interest will be less than $1,000 for the first thirteen years of $30,000 in 8 percent bonds due in eighteen years. You could thus buy taxable zeros for a young child and keep the taxes low for the life of the bond.

343 CONSIDER TAX-DEFERRED OR TAX-EXEMPT INVESTMENTS.

A suitable tax-deferred investment you might put into a child's name: Series EE bonds (see Chapter Seven). You might also purchase a single-premium life insurance policy for yourself or your spouse, and borrow against it to pay for a child's education (see Chapter Eight). The cash value in an insurance policy, by the way, doesn't count as part of your assets when colleges ponder whether your child needs financial help.

If you're not far from fifty-nine and a half, or if the grandparents are interested, you or they might purchase an annuity, withdrawing the investment to pay for a child's education. You usually must pay a 10 percent penalty on the withdrawal if you take out money from the annuity before you're fifty-nine and a half.

Other suitable tax-exempt investments include municipal bonds, municipal bond mutual funds, municipal bond unit trusts, and zero-coupon municipal bonds.

344   CONSIDER AN IRREVOCABLE TRUST.

People setting up new trusts will have the income taxed at their own tax rates if the trust money ever reverts to them, or if they can control the trust in any way. But you can still have trust money taxed to the trust if you give up all your rights to your gift—the gift is irrevocable.

Trusts are taxed at a rate of 15 percent on the first $5,000 of income, and above that at 28 percent. (The benefit of the 15 percent rate is phased out by a surcharge as income grows from $13,000 to $26,000.) Those rates may be lower than yours.

Another possible benefit of a trust: You can put real estate into it—which you cannot always do with a custodial account.

With a 2503(c) trust, the money is turned over to the child when he or she reaches eighteen or twenty-one, depending on the law in your state. A lawyer may charge a few hundred dollars to set up such a trust.

345   GIVE A CHILD (OR A SPOUSE) A JOB.

If you're self-employed, or you have a part-time free-lance job, hire your child. You'll keep money in the family that way.

Pay the child a reasonable wage—not ridiculously high—and you can deduct it from your own income. And the money will be taxed at the child's rate even if the tyke is under fourteen. If the child earns less than $2,450 in 1987 or under $3,000 in 1988, none of the earned income will be taxed. (While a child's unearned income is offset by a standard deduction of only $500, the standard deduction for earned income can go as high as $3,000 in 1988.)

You need not pay Social Security taxes for a child under

twenty-one (or a spouse who works for you) if your business isn't incorporated, although that rule might change soon.

A physician paid his children to answer the phone in his office and file papers; the IRS objected to his deducting their salaries, but a tax court approved. A writer I know pays his son to do library research for him; a computer programmer has his boy work on various projects—and claims the kid does a better job than he does.

Just don't try getting away with deducting the cost of paying a child to do his or her homework.

Even if your child works for you, you can claim the child as an exemption if he or she is under nineteen or a full-time student, and you provide more than half the total support.

346 FUND A CHILD'S IRA.

If a child has earned income, he or she can put up to $2,000 of the amount into an Individual Retirement Arrangement. That way, he or she may avoid taxes on income below $5,000 (the $2,000 IRA and the $3,000 standard deduction for 1988), and probably be very wealthy when he or she retires.

If a person puts away $2,000 into an IRA from age nineteen to twenty-six, and STOPS, he or she will have $1,035,160 at age 65 (assuming the money compounded at 10 percent a year). If the person starts at age twenty-seven, and CONTINUES putting $2,000 into an IRA every year until he or she is sixty-five, he or she will have less— $883,185. In short, the younger you begin an IRA investment program, the better.

An investment adviser, Paul Merriman of Seattle, recently became a grandfather. The baby is being paid to model. Merriman suggested that the baby's $2,000 be salted away into an IRA, and provide a rich inheritance for the child later in life.

347 CONSIDER "TUITION FUTURES."

Around a dozen colleges now offer "tuition plans." Years in advance, you pay the tuition for your child's college education, at a bargain rate. (Duquesne University in Pittsburgh started the first such plan, in 1985.) The IRS hasn't ruled on whether the parents should be taxed on the earnings in the plan.

Someday, though, "tuition futures" may be common. Many states are even considering offering tuition futures for students who want to attend any public college or university in their state.

348 GET SOCIAL SECURITY NUMBERS FOR YOUR DEPENDENTS OVER FOUR.

Otherwise, you'll face a penalty of $5 per child.

349 HAVE THE LOWER-EARNING DIVORCÉ(E) CLAIM THE CHILD DEPENDENCY.

Consider having the lower-earning parent claim the child as a dependent. Reason: Beginning in 1988, high-earners gradually lose personal exemptions for themselves and their children as their income climbs. But the lower-earning parent may still benefit. In the past, the higher-earning parent usually wanted the exemption, because he or she was in a higher tax bracket.

350 CONSIDER A NEW ALIMONY ARRANGEMENT.

Before tax reform, you could deduct $10,000 for alimony you paid; anything beyond $10,000 was deductible only if you were required to make payments for six or more years.

Now you can deduct as much as $15,000 a year; amounts over that are deductible if they're made for at least three years, and are regular enough not to look like lump-sum payments.

What this means is that you can arrange to make more generous payments over a shorter period of time, boosting your early deductions. And remember that alimony you pay lowers your adjusted gross income—which helps you itemize, and helps you surpass the floors for medical expenses, casualty losses, and certain miscellaneous expenses.

351 BE WARY OF RECEIVING PROPERTY IN A DIVORCE.

If you receive property—say, a house—you won't have to pay income taxes when you receive it. But when you sell, you'll pay—and your basis (total investment) will be the price of the house when your spouse purchased it, not the date you received it. And remember that capital-gains taxes are going up to the rates on ordinary income. Cash might be better, because you would pay less taxes on account of the decline in tax rates. So, if your ex wants to give you property, ask for extra concessions.

If you're making the alimony payments, though, you may prefer to give property. Reason: Less of your alimony payments are deductible now that tax rates are going down.

So you and your ex may have some serious talking to do. Many existing divorce decrees and separation agreements can be renegotiated when there's a big change in the tax law.

352 MAKE SURE THAT YOUR ALIMONY PAYMENTS ARE DEDUCTIBLE.

The rules governing divorce decrees and separate-maintenance agreements before 1985 differ from those later on.

For payments under a decree of divorce or agreement AFTER 1984 to be deductible, payments must be in cash, not in property.

353 CONSIDER FUNDING AN IRA WITH ALIMONY YOU RECEIVE.

You're allowed to fund an individual retirement arrangement with the alimony you receive, as if it were earned income. (And I'm not implying it's not!)

354 DON'T GIVE YOUR EX-SPOUSE AN ANNUITY.

It won't qualify as alimony because it's considered property, and you cannot deduct property as alimony. But the paying spouse could obtain an annuity, give the payments he or she receives to the ex-spouse, then deduct the payments as alimony.

355 REMEMBER THAT YOU CAN BE FLEXIBLE.

Normally, alimony you pay is deductible; alimony you receive is taxable. But what if the paying spouse wants to be generous—and not deduct the alimony, and not have the ex-spouse pay taxes on it as income?

That can be arranged. The divorce decree or separation agreement can specify that a payment won't qualify as alimony for tax purposes, and the IRS will go along.

356 DEDUCT LEGAL COSTS ...

of a divorce insofar as they were for obtaining alimony payments, or for tax advice. They are miscellaneous expenses, subject to the floor of 2 percent of your adjusted gross income. You can also deduct the cost of getting your ex-spouse to make the payments he or she owes.

357 DEDUCT THE ENTIRE AMOUNT OF ALIMONY . . .

even if part of it goes for child support, so long as your legal arrangement didn't specify that a certain portion go to any children.

Chapter Fourteen
RETIREMENT

For many people, contributions to individual retirement arrangements are no longer deductible—and that has led to one of the most vexing questions post–tax reform: Should you open up a nondeductible IRA?

Tax reform has also lowered the maximum you can contribute to a salary-reduction plan, and cut back on the special income-averaging of lump-sum pension distributions. But there are a few pluses, too. Now you can withdraw money from an IRA before age fifty-nine and a half, without penalty, if you "annuitize" the payments—receive them in line with your projected life span. And if your spouse earns less than $250, you can put an extra $250 into a spousal IRA. (Before tax reform, if your spouse earned—say—$150, you could put only $150 into a spousal IRA.) Other new wrinkles are reported below.

358 FUND A RETIREMENT PLAN.

Here's a reason you may not have thought of: Whatever you can deduct from your gross income (adjustments like deductible IRA contributions) lowers the floors to let you deduct more medical expenses, more casualty losses, and more miscellaneous deductions. Overall, that also enables you to itemize all your deductions rather than opt for the fixed standard deduction.

Of course, the key benefit of a retirement plan is that your contributions will grow, tax-deferred; and, while you may be in the 28 percent or 33 percent bracket in 1988, you might be in the 15 percent bracket years from now, when you withdraw your money—and thus save a bundle on the total taxes you pay. It's also possible that you can fund your pension plan with pre-tax dollars, as with a deductible IRA or a salary-reduction (401[k]) plan.

People keep wondering how to invest retirement money. My general advice is: If you're young, consider stocks. Stocks, in the long run, have performed far better than bonds and money-market instruments. But note that I said "in the long run." If you're young, you can wait out the usual stomach-turning stock-market declines. I recommend that young people invest in no-load stock mutual funds with good long-term records.

But if you're getting on in years, you should probably tilt toward fixed-interest investments, like bonds or certificates of deposit. You don't want to find yourself needing the money to live on, just when the stock market is in the doldrums. Vary your bonds' maturities: Have some short-term, some middle-term, some long-term. Short-term usually means a year to five years; middle-term, five to seven years; and long-term is anything over that. If you need every cent from your pension, and can't afford any risk whatever, consider money-market funds. Inflation can shrink the money you have even in short-term bonds.

Still, a good case can be made for diversifying. Young people might purchase fixed-return investments, especially if they're not familiar with the ups and downs of the stock market, and might panic in a downturn; older people not in straitened circumstances might have some good stocks or stock mutual funds, along with their fixed-income invest-ments. Stocks and stock mutual funds offer some protection against inflation; they offer the greatest possibility of appreciation; and they're fun to follow. Just remember: The worst mistake you can make when you buy stocks is to panic when the market goes down and sell your holdings.

359 FUND A 401(K) PLAN.

Salary-reduction or 401(k) plans are absolutely wonderful—better even than deductible IRAs. You can put more money away—up to $7,000 (as of 1987; the amount will rise with the Consumer Price Index) or 20 percent of your income, whichever is less. Your contribution is automatically deducted from your salary; and while it's subject to Social Security taxes, it's immune to current income taxes. (This isn't true of other employer-sponsored thrift or profit-sharing plans, in which your contributions are made with post-tax money.) You can even borrow some of your investment, which you can't do with an IRA.

As if all these benefits weren't enough, many employers kick in a contribution of their own, typically as high as 50 percent of your contribution, though perhaps up to a cutoff point.

Beg or borrow (draw the line at stealing), but do fund your 401(k) plan. I meet people who say they can't afford to contribute. They can't afford not to. They should sell other assets, or borrow from relatives or friends. If your employer kicks in 20 percent, or 50 percent, a 401(k) is too tempting to pass up.

Your $7,000 limit (as of 1987) doesn't include your employer's contribution. But your employer's contribution DOES count toward the limit of 20 percent of your salary. (Most people I know put away 5–15 percent.) In fact, if you also have access to a Simplified Employee Pension where you work, your contributions to the SEP count toward your current total $7,000 limit, as do contributions you make to other employer-sponsored retirement arrangements.

Borrowing from your 401(k) plan should be done only with the best of reasons—like buying a house. The rules are a bit complicated.

Tax reform requires you to pay back your loan within five years, unless you're borrowing to buy a home for yourself (not for a child or other relative). You must repay the loan in level quarterly installments. If you borrow $5,000, you must repay $1,000 a year, $250 every four months.

The old rule was that you could borrow half your pension assets, up to $50,000; but you could always borrow $10,000.

Now the amount you can borrow depends on what you've borrowed in the previous twelve months.

Let's say you have $100,000 in your plan (lucky you), and you theoretically could borrow half, or $50,000. You've borrowed $40,000, then repaid it. But within the next year, you borrow another $10,000. Now you want to borrow more.

Take the $50,000 limit, and subtract: $40,000 minus $10,000, or $30,000. You can borrow $20,000. Before tax reform, you could have borrowed $40,000 (the $50,000 limit minus the existing $10,000 loan).

Obviously, the IRS wants to discourage frequent borrowings from pension plans.

The rules on withdrawing money from 401(k)s before age fifty-nine and a half are strict. You can permanently take out your assets for "financial hardship," if you leave the company, or if you're disabled. "Financial hardship" hasn't been defined by the IRS, but it might encompass the need to buy a house.

If you withdraw money from a 401(k) for financial hardship, you'll have to pay a 10 percent penalty on the amount you withdraw, along with regular income taxes. Exception: If your withdrawal is to pay for medical expenses that qualify as tax-deductible, there's no penalty. (But starting in 1989, you cannot withdraw your earnings on your contributions.)

You can use special income-averaging on withdrawals if (a) you're fifty-nine and a half, (b) you take a lump-sum distribution, and (3) you belonged to the plan for at least five years.

360 PERSUADE YOUR EMPLOYER TO START A 401(K) PLAN.

Explain that such a plan will help your company keep its valuable employees, and lure new valuable employees. More and more job seekers inquire about 401(k) plans. It amazes and appalls me that some small companies still offer no pension plan at all.

361 FUND A DEDUCTIBLE IRA.

Even if your salary is $11 million, like Lee Iacocca of Chrysler, you can deduct your IRA contribution SO LONG AS YOU WERE NOT AN ACTIVE MEMBER OF A QUALIFIED EMPLOYER-SPONSORED PENSION PLAN. Such plans include 401(k) plans; pension, profit-sharing, and stock-bonus plans; Keoghs or HR-10s; annuity plans; Simplified Employee Benefit Plans; and 501(c)(18) union pension plans.

If you or your spouse participate in a company retirement plan, you can still deduct your IRA contribution if your adjusted gross income was $40,000 or less. If you're single or a head of household, the cutoff is $35,000. If you're married, you can deduct SOME of your IRA contribution if your adjusted gross income is less than $50,000; the same is true of a single person whose adjusted gross income is below $35,000. In calculating your adjusted gross income, do NOT subtract your IRA contributions.

For every $1 your adjusted gross income exceeds $40,000/$25,000, you lose 20 cents of your deduction. Let's say your adjusted gross income is $46,000 and you're filing jointly. You're $6,000 above the limit. Multiply the $6,000 by 20 cents, to get $1,200. Subtract that from $2,000—and you wind up with the amount you can deduct, $800. (But you still can put $1,200—$2,000 minus $800—into a NONDEDUCTIBLE IRA.) Suppose your adjusted gross income is $49,000. Multiply $9,000 by 20 cents, and you get $1,800. You can deduct only $200.

The most you can salt away into an IRA during one year, for yourself, is $2,000, or 100 percent of your earned income, whichever is less. Dividends, interest, capital gains, and such don't qualify as earned income, though alimony and separate-maintenance agreements do.

Okay, a key question is: Are you or aren't you a participant in a qualified retirement plan? If you elect to join a 401(k) plan and part of your salary is deferred, you're a participant. In fact, you don't have to actively participate to be considered a participant in a plan; if you're eligible, you're ineligible for a deductible IRA. So is your spouse, even if he/she isn't covered.

If you belong to a profit-sharing plan, though, and there were no profits that went your way, you're not a participant. The same is true if you're in a stock-bonus plan, and received no stock.

Check with your employer if you're not sure whether or not you actively participate in a plan. And you MAY not be sure if you left your place of employment during the year.

You cannot invest your IRA in collectibles, antiques, art, stamps, or precious metals. An exception: gold or silver coins issued by the government.

By April 1 of the year after you reach seventy and a half, you must start withdrawing your money from your IRAs. If you take out money in installments, it must all have been withdrawn by the end of your estimated life span. (Your IRA's custodian will have tables showing estimated life spans.) If you're married, you can use the longer life spans based on your life expectancy together with your spouse's.

You cannot contribute to an IRA past the time you reach

seventy and a half. But if your spouse is under seventy and a half and unemployed, you can continue contributing on his or her behalf.

362 DON'T PUT SHORT-TERM MONEY INTO AN IRA.

Put money into an IRA only if you're pretty sure you won't be needing it till you're at least fifty-nine and a half. If you withdraw your IRA funds prematurely (you're not fifty-nine and a half or disabled, or you don't take the payments in amounts geared to your estimated life span), you face a 10 percent tax penalty on the amount you withdraw, along with regular income taxes. (You won't pay taxes on your principal if you withdraw funds from a nondeductible IRA. But if you have both deductible and nondeductible IRAs, any withdrawal is considered to come partially from both.) You would have to keep an IRA for many years—about thirteen—before your earnings would overcome that 10 percent penalty.

363 DON'T PUT TAX-EXEMPT INVESTMENTS INTO AN IRA.

Yes, some people put tax-free municipal bonds into IRAs. This is redundant, because IRA contributions grow tax-deferred anyway. It's also disastrous: Whatever you withdraw from an IRA is taxed as if it were ordinary income. So your tax-free municipal-bond interest would be taxed as soon as it left your IRA!

364 BORROW TO FUND YOUR IRA.

All of the interest on a loan to fund an IRA is deductible, the IRS has ruled. That gives you an incentive to borrow to

fund your IRA, if you don't have the money available—
particularly if your IRA contribution itself is still deductible.

But with the lowering of tax brackets, this step may not
make as much financial sense as before. You don't save as
much taxes as you used to, when tax brackets were higher.
You must consider the interest, dividends, and possible
capital gains from your IRA.

So rather than borrowing from a bank, find a really cheap
source of money, like a loan from any whole-life insurance
policy you have. An even cheaper source: borrowing from
yourself. Roll over an existing IRA; use the money to fund
your new IRA; then, when you have more money, put the
amount you withdrew into the rollover IRA. Do it within
sixty days of your borrowing the money, so you won't have
a tax penalty.

365 TAKE THE $200 IRA DEDUCTION.

Let's say that you're married, filing a joint return, and your
adjusted gross income is $49,500. Poor you, according to
the calculations—you can deduct only $100. The IRA,
though, lets you deduct $200—just as long as your adjusted
gross income is below $50,000. Remember this break if your
adjusted gross income is over $49,000 for 1987. And if
you're single or the head of a household, remember the $200
deduction if your adjusted gross income is over $34,000.

366 FUND A SPOUSAL IRA.

You work, earning at least $2,250 a year, but your spouse
doesn't work at all. Or you work, but your spouse earns less
than $250 a year. The result is that you can salt away
$2,250 into a deductible IRA. You can put $2,000 in your
name, or in your spouse's name; or put $1,175 in each of
your names. But you cannot put more than $2,000 into one

account. If it's a nondeductible IRA, you might put most of it into the IRA of the spouse with not many deductible IRAs. That way, you can withdraw the principal before you're fifty-nine and a half, and pay less of a penalty because you've withdrawn proportionately less from deductible IRAs.

Also consider persuading a working child to set up an IRA.

And think about hiring your spouse, so he/she can fund an IRA—which may be deductible if you're not a member of a qualified employer-sponsored retirement plan. Some sole proprietors hire their spouses to help out in the office, paying them at least $2,000 a year. A free-lance writer I know has his wife research some of his articles, and pays her for exactly $2,000 worth of work. ("She's a lousy researcher," he says.)

367 DEDUCT CUSTODIAL FEES.

You can deduct fees you pay a custodian during the year to manage your IRA if they are "ordinary and necessary." They're "miscellaneous" deductions, subject to a reduction of 2 percent of your adjusted gross income.

368 TRANSFER YOUR IRAS FOR HIGHER RETURNS.

At IRA time (January to April 15), some banks offer certificates of deposit paying high interest. Then, once they have lured lots of IRA money, they let their interest rates sink, compared to what other banks are paying, trusting that depositors will remain with them, out of inertia. But you can transfer your account from custodian to custodian as often as you like, as long as you yourself don't have access to the money. So ask a bank paying a competitive interest rate to handle the transfer. That will spare you some paperwork—

and enable you to transfer your IRA again the same year, if you like. And remember: You aren't limited to banks in your area. In fact, you aren't limited to banks. Consider stockbrokers and mutual funds.

You can make as many IRA transfers as you like; but you're limited to one rollover per account a year (in a rollover, you get direct access to the funds).

369 CONSIDER A NONDEDUCTIBLE IRA.

Why not a municipal-bond fund instead? Good question. A muni fund would be liquid—you could get the money if you needed it, without tax penalties. And when you retrieve all your interest, you wouldn't pay a penny in taxes—whereas the interest and appreciation on an IRA investment would be taxed as regular income.

There are two arguments in favor of nondeductible IRAs: (1) You can earn more on your money. Corporate bonds, for example, pay more than munis—and they can be just as safe or safer, if you stick with high-rated issues. In fact, if you put a nondeductible IRA in a growth or aggressive-growth mutual fund with a good record, like Twentieth Century Select or Fidelity Magellan, you may make out like a bandit—and all of your gains will be tax-deferred. (2) You may not want such easy access to your money. A friend says, "I started a muni fund for my spouse, as part of her retirement money. Then the house needed aluminum siding . . . the kid wanted to take a summer course at the Center for Academically Talented Youth . . . and my dentist discovered a gold mine of periodontal work in my mouth. Bye-bye, muni fund. If the money had been locked up in an IRA, I might not have withdrawn it so readily."

Of course, there's nothing wrong with having a liquid municipal-bond fund—along with a nondeductible IRA in a higher-paying investment.

370 INCOME-AVERAGE A LUMP-SUM DISTRIBUTION.

If you leave your employer and receive all of your pension-plan assets in one lump sum, there's a way to avoid being taxed on the entire amount at your highest tax rate.

Before tax reform, you would calculate the tax on one-tenth the amount, multiply it by ten, and that was your onetime tax on the distribution. Confused? Remember, there were lots of tax brackets way back when. One-tenth of the distribution very likely fell into a low tax bracket. Multiplying that tax by ten was probably far less than the tax on the entire amount, at the higher tax bracket.

Tax reform, though, abolished that special break—unless you were fifty years old or older on January 1, 1986. In that case, you can choose between ten-year averaging and five-year averaging of a lump-sum distribution. (If you're below fifty-nine and a half, you can never use this break again.)

The choice between ten-year averaging and five-year averaging isn't simple. Ten-year averaging is based on the higher tax rates of 1986; five-year averaging is based on the new, lower tax rates. You'll have to figure it out both ways to see which is better for you.

Those who weren't at least fifty on that date can choose only five-year income averaging. Your tax on a lump-sum distribution is five times what the tax is on one-fifth the distribution. Let's hope that, in 1988, one-fifth of any distribution you receive falls within the 15 percent bracket, and not the 28 percent or the 33 percent brackets. You can use five-year averaging only once, and only after you've reached fifty-nine and a half.

371 AVOID THE 10 PERCENT PENALTY ON LUMP-SUM DISTRIBUTIONS.

You'll face that penalty if you withdraw your pension money before you're fifty-nine and a half, even if the reason is that you've left your job. (But there's no penalty if you withdrew the money because you were disabled.)

One solution: You can roll over the money into an IRA (see below). Or, if you get a new job, you can roll over the lump sum into your new employer's pension plan, if you have your new employer's permission. Or, if you've left your job, you can choose to have the lump sum taken as an annuity. Finally, if you're at least fifty and take early retirement under your company's plan, the penalty doesn't apply.

372 HAVE YOUR DISTRIBUTION TAXED AS CAPITAL GAINS.

Before tax reform, if you had contributions to your pension plan before 1974, you could treat that part of your distribution as a long-term gain, which is taxed leniently. You figured out the ratio of pre-1974 investment years and your post-1974 investment years.

Now this favorable treatment of pre-1974 gains is being phased out. If you take out your pension money in 1987, all of your pre-1974 gains are taxed leniently. In 1988, it's 95 percent. In 1989, it's 75 percent. In 1990, it's 50 percent. In 1991, it's 25 percent. In 1992, the special break vanishes entirely. But if you were fifty or more on January 1, 1986, all of the pre-1974 contributions will still be taxed leniently—whatever the year you receive your distributions. The tax rate will be a straight 20 percent; it doesn't vary according to your tax bracket.

373 ROLL OVER A DISTRIBUTION.

You leave your job, or your company goes out of business. Right now, you don't need the $50,000 (or whatever) the company gives you, and you don't expect to need it over the next few years. You don't want to pay taxes on it, and you do want it to continue appreciating. Your best course is to roll over the distribution into an IRA. (Lump sums aren't subject to the usual $2,000 limit.) There's no tax bite if you do it within sixty days of your getting the distribution. Inform your new custodian—bank, savings and loan, stockbroker, mutual fund—that this is a rollover IRA.

Warning: By rolling over a lump-sum distribution, you lose the right ever to use special income averaging on the distribution. Money withdrawn from an IRA cannot be income-averaged. But if you won't need the money for years, a rollover will still usually give you more money in the long run.

374 CONSIDER A KEOGH.

The self-employed should consider Keogh plans, or HR-10 plans, as the IRS prefers them to be known.

You can deduct your contribution from your income. And your contributions grow, tax-free.

You must set up a Keogh before the end of the year, though; you cannot contribute to one in 1988 unless you made the arrangements in 1987—although you can do that with a Simplified Employee Pension plan or an IRA.

Among the types of Keoghs:

DEFINED CONTRIBUTION

With a profit-sharing plan, you can put in whichever is lower: up to $30,000 every year, or up to 15 percent of your earnings (minus pension-plan contributions). Here's how to figure out your Keogh contribution: Multiply your net earned income by 15 percent; divide the result by 1.15. That's your maximum, providing it's not over $30,000. Example: You netted $50,000. Multiply that by 15 percent, which gives you $7,500. Dividing by 1.15 gives you $6,521—your deductible contribution. Or just multiply the net earned income by 13.043.

With a profit-sharing plan, you can vary the amounts you put into your Keogh.

With a money-purchase plan, you can contribute 20 percent of your net earnings. Here, you divide by 1.2. If you net $50,000, you can contribute $8,333 ($50,000 times 20 percent divided by 1.2). Or just multiply your net earned income by 16.66.

With a money-purchase plan, you must contribute a fixed percentage of your income every year.

DEFINED BENEFIT

This is a lot more complicated than a defined-contribution plan. What you contribute depends upon what you'd like to withdraw every year when you retire, and that amount will depend upon your life expectancy. The annual benefit when you retire can't exceed more than $90,000—or your average earnings for the three consecutive working years during which you earned the most money.

Tax reform has lowered the income you receive from a defined-benefit plan if you retire earlier than sixty-five.

The trouble with defined-benefit plans is that they lock you into making a set contribution—whether you can afford it or not. They're best for people getting on in years, who can afford several years of high payments.

You must start withdrawing your Keogh money by age fifty-nine and a half, either in installments or all at once. If you withdraw your money in a lump sum, you can take advantage of the special income-averaging formula.

You can fund a Keogh—or a SEP (see below)—even if you're salaried, so long as you also have some self-employment income.

375 DEFER FUNDING YOUR KEOGH.

You don't have enough money to fund a Keogh? If you file early, you can nonetheless deduct for a Keogh contribution—and, if you have tax money coming to you, use the refund to finally fund your plan. (The IRS trusts you.)

Or you can file for a two-month automatic extension of

the due date of your return, meanwhile paying all of your tax bill. Then you'll have an extra two months to fund your Keogh. This extension tactic doesn't work with IRAs or Simplified Employee Pensions.

376 CONSIDER A SEP.

If you're self-employed, you can set up a SEP, which doesn't have the onerous reporting requirements of a Keogh. Another advantage: You can establish a SEP a year after the year your contribution was for—in 1988, you can set up and contribute to a SEP for 1987. A SEP, like an IRA, can be only a defined-contribution plan, not a defined-benefit plan.

With a SEP, you can contribute 15 pecent of your net self-employment income (minus your contribution), up to $30,000. The percentage winds up being 13.043 percent.

Employers can set up SEPs for their workers if they have twenty-five or fewer employees, and at least half participate. Such an SEP works like an IRA.

Unlike lump-sum distributions from a Keogh, those from a SEP don't qualify for special income averaging. And even if you file for an extension to submit your tax return, you must make your SEP contribution by April 15—again, unlike a Keogh.

Chapter Fifteen
ALTERNATE
MINIMUM TAX

The alternate minimum tax is a "shadow" tax system. If you or your tax adviser have been so clever that you've shrunk your normal taxes way, way down, the AMT kicks in. Certain exclusions and deductions that were allowed when you figured out your taxes the regular way will now be taxed. You must calculate your taxes the regular way, then see if you've been so resourceful in avoiding taxes that you're subject to the AMT. If you are, you'll pay a higher tax.

Predictions are that more people will be whacked with the AMT thanks to tax reform.

First, there are more tax breaks that set you up for the AMT.

Second, the exemption of a chunk of the income of very well-to-do people from the AMT is being reduced. The exemption is normally $40,000 on a joint return, $30,000 for single people. But now, for every dollar of AMT income above $150,000 (if you're single, $112,500), you lose 25 cents of the exemption. The exemption is eliminated for joint returns at $310,000, for singles at $232,500.

Third, the AMT tax rate has gone up from a flat rate of

20 percent to 21 percent. That may not seem very high. But when you recall that the highest rates in 1988 and after are only 28 percent and 33 percent, you can see that the AMT will kick in sooner. It's not hard to use tax breaks to lower your overall tax rate significantly below 28 percent or 33 percent—and thus have reduced your overall tax rate below the trigger point, 21 percent.

Despite the predictions, it's possible that the AMT may not ensnare all that many taxpayers. In the past, the favorable treatment of long-term capital gains tripped up a great many people. But now that long-term gains are being taxed like ordinary income, a dangerous AMT trap is being closed. Even though in 1987 you'll pay no more than a 28 percent rate on such gains, whereas the top tax rate is 38.5 percent, the 5 percent difference won't set you up for the AMT.

Here's how you figure out the AMT:

1. Take your adjusted gross income from Form 1040.
2. Recalculate certain items, such as for depreciation.
3. Add back your "tax preference" items.
4. Subtract the itemized deductions still allowed for the AMT.
5. You now have your "alternative minimum taxable income" (AMTI).
6. Subtract the exemption you're allowed ($40,000 for a married couple filing jointly, for example).
7. You now have the amount subject to the AMT.
8. Multiply it by 21 percent.
9. If the result is more than your regular tax, it's what you pay instead of the regular tax.

Tax breaks that set you up for the AMT are called "preferences." Some preferences are common, some rare. Among them: any deduction you've taken for the growth in the value of property (like stocks) you've given to a charity; any accelerated depreciation on real property and leased personal property, after 1986, above what would have been allowed under straight-line method; the value of real-estate depreciation deductions, after 1986, above the value of forty-year depreciation; the tax benefit of installment sales; the value of stock options when you exercise them; the value of mining exploration and development costs; percentage depletion allowances; intangible drilling and development costs from oil and gas properties.

To calculate your AMT income, you must also give back many tax breaks you've taken advantage of:

• Consumer interest—on credit cards, car loans, student loans—that you've deducted. For 1987, you can deduct 65 percent; for 1988, 40 percent. For the AMT, add back those percentages. All consumer interest is prey to the AMT.

• Investment interest beyond your investment income. Under the AMT, you get no partial deduction for any excess.

• A variety of itemized deductions, including state and local income taxes, real-estate taxes, and medical expenses below 10 percent (not 7.5 percent, as with regular deductions) of your adjusted gross income.

• Any "passive" income losses you've deducted under the phaseout rules (for example, 65 percent for 1987, 40 percent for 1988). For the AMT, you get no breaks on passive-income losses. (Passive income comes from investments like limited partnerships.) But you can carry forward disallowed passive losses to a future year when you have offsetting passive income.

• Deductions for contributions of property (like stocks) that have gone up in value and that you've given to charity. Normally, you can claim the appreciated value of your gift. For the AMT, add back the appreciation.

• Miscellaneous itemized deductions (like employee business expenses), including those that surpassed 2 percent of your adjusted gross income.

• Interest on certain "non-essential" or "private activity"

nongovernmental tax-exempt bonds issued after August 7, 1986.

• The foreign tax credit: Under the new rules, it's now limited to 90 percent of your minimum-tax liability.

If you have ANY tax-preference items, the IRS says, you must submit Form 6251—even if you aren't subject to the AMT!

377 REMEMBER DEDUCTIONS YOU STILL CAN TAKE.

Among them: medical expenses above 10 percent of your adjusted gross income; charitable contributions, not including carryovers; casualty losses; gambling losses; investment interest to the extent of your investment income; and home mortgage interest (but not interest against the appreciation of your home, even if you used the money for education or medical expenses). You CAN deduct interest on a mortgage to build or rehabilitate your main home, though. But if you refinance your mortgage for more than the original balance, the interest on the additional loan isn't deductible from AMT income.

378 SUBTRACT THOSE DEDUCTIONS EVEN IF YOU DON'T ITEMIZE.

If you didn't itemize but took the standard deduction in doing your tax the regular way, you can still take allowable itemized deductions from your AMT income.

379 DON'T ADD BACK THE "EXPENSING" DEDUCTION.

The Section 179 ("expensing") deduction on new personal property, up to $10,000, isn't a tax-preference item.

380 BEWARE OF "NON-ESSENTIAL" BONDS.

Make sure your broker doesn't buy you "private activity" or "non-essential" municipal bonds subject to the AMT without warning you. A tip-off: Such bonds pay higher interest than bonds not subject to the AMT.

381 TRY TO KEEP PASSIVE-LOSS DEDUCTIONS.

In 1987 you can still write off 65 percent of passive losses against active and against portfolio income; in 1988, 40 percent. So, if during any of these phaseout years you have large passive losses, and insufficient passive gains to match them with, try especially hard to avoid the AMT—which would eliminate any passive-loss deductions altogether.

In fact, over the next few years, try to avoid the AMT—or you'll lose other partially available deductions, including consumer interest and investment interest above investment income.

382 TRY TO KEEP HOUSING CREDITS.

Steer clear of the AMT in years when you're entitled to the low-income housing or rehabilitative-housing credit. They cannot be used to lower your AMT.

383 SHIFT INCOME AND DEDUCTIONS TO AVOID THE AMT.

Hold off giving appreciated property to a charity until a year when you'll be safe from the AMT. Avoid installment sales if they might trigger the AMT. Try to depreciate certain assets according to their usable life, not the scheduled five- to seven-year depreciation periods—so as to avoid the adjustment otherwise required by the AMT. Time the exercise of stock options, to avoid years when you may be subject to the tax.

If you're planning to give appreciated property to a charity NEXT year, and you may be hit by the AMT, consider making your contribution this year—along with other deductions, like medical expenses and consumer interest. If you're subject to the AMT, you won't benefit from those deductions.

384 CONSIDER HAVING MORE INCOME SUBJECT TO THE AMT.

A 21 percent AMT is a better rate than 28 percent or 33 percent. So, consider pushing income into an AMT year—a year when you're enjoying bounteous tax breaks. Sell an asset for a gain; redeem government savings bonds; ask for a bonus earlier than scheduled.

385 REMEMBER AMT CREDITS YOU'RE ENTITLED TO.

Someday, because of accelerated depreciation, you'll have to pay more taxes. And the extra value of those stock options you exercised will finally be taxed—their value will be added to your investment when you sell. The IRS has understood this, so you can get a special AMT benefit in years when your regular tax is more than your AMT.

Recompute your AMT, adding back only itemized deductions, percentage depletion, tax-exempt interest, and appreciated-property charitable deductions. The difference between this AMT and the official AMT becomes a credit you can carry forward to future years, when you aren't subject to the AMT.

Appendix A
Tax Rates for 1987 and 1988

Taxable Income	Tax Rates	
Married–Joint Return		
	1987	*1988*
0–$3,000	11%	15%
$3,001–$28,000	15%	15%
$28,001–$29,750	28%	15%
$29,751–$45,000	28%	28%
$45,001–$71,900	35%	28%
$71,901–$90,000	35%	33%
Above $90,000	38.5%	33%*
Single Return		
0–$1,800	11%	15%
$1,801–$16,800	15%	15%
$16,801–$17,850	28%	28%
$17,851–$27,000	28%	28%
$27,001–$43,150	35%	28%
$43,151–$54,000	35%	33%
Above $54,000	38.5%	33%*
Head of Household		
0–$2,500	11%	15%
$2,501–$23,000	15%	
$2,501–$23,900		15%
$23,001–$38,000	28%	
$23,901–$61,650		28%
$38,001–$80,000	35%	
Above $61,650		33%*
Above $80,000	38.5%	

*The marginal tax rate retreats to 28% when taxable income exceeds certain amounts—the exact amount depending upon the number of personal exemptions the taxpayer claims. The 33% rate is to eliminate the benefit of the 15% rate and personal exemptions.

Appendix B

INVESTING IN MUTUAL FUNDS WITH AND WITHOUT INSURANCE

	Variable Life	Variable Annuity	No-Load Mutual Funds	Individual Retirement Account
TAXATION	Earnings grow, tax deferred.	Earnings grow, tax deferred.	Distributions are taxed; appreciation is tax deferred.	Earnings grow, tax deferred.
WITHDRAWALS	No tax penalty.	Usually 10% tax penalty before age 59½.	No tax penalty.	Usually 10% tax penalty before age 59½.
EXCHANGES BETWEEN FUNDS	Not taxed.	Not taxed.	Taxable.	Not taxed.
LOANS	Not taxed.	Taxable.	Not applicable.	Taxable.
INVESTMENT CHOICES	Limited.	Limited.	Many.	Many.
SURRENDER CHARGES	Has either a declining percentage or front-end charge.	Usually a declining percentage.	Usually none.	Usually none.
TYPICAL TOTAL EXPENSES	2% a year, plus cost of insurance.	2% a year.	1.5% a year.	1.5% a year.
TAXATION AT DEATH	All proceeds not taxed.	Appreciation—not principal—taxed as ordinary income.	All proceeds not subject to income tax (but perhaps estate tax).	Appreciation taxed as ordinary income.

INDEX